AF521812

Art & Artifice

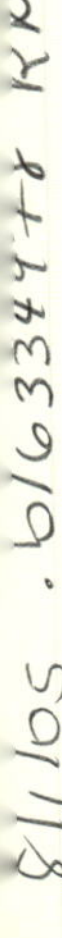

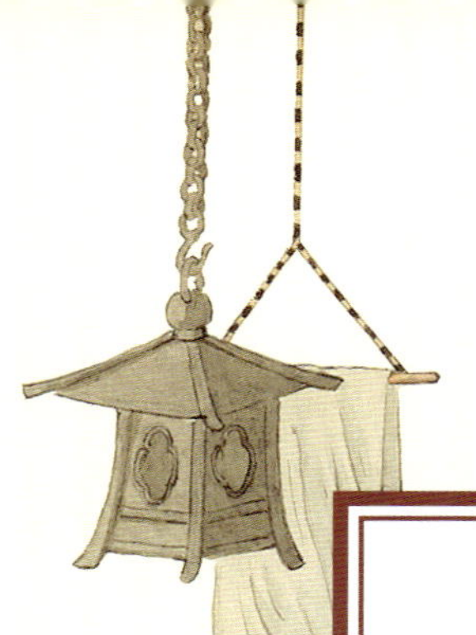

Art & Artifice

JAPANESE PHOTOGRAPHS OF THE MEIJI ERA

Selections from the Jean S. and Frederic A. Sharf Collection

at the Museum of Fine Arts, Boston

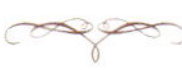

with essays by

Sebastian Dobson, Anne Nishimura Morse, and Frederic A. Sharf

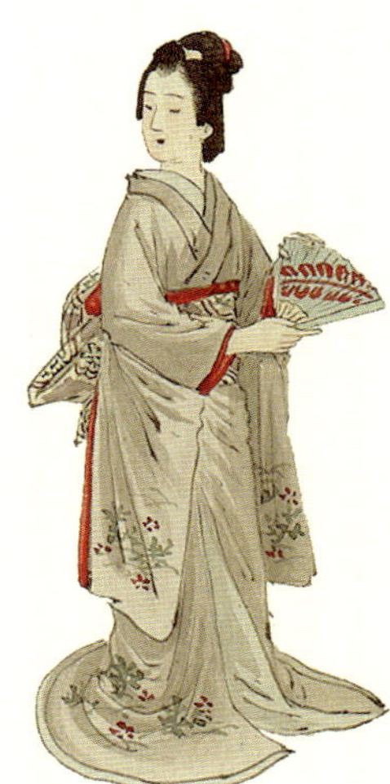

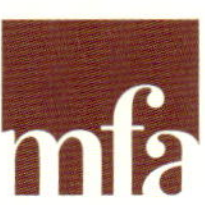

MFA PUBLICATIONS

a division of the Museum of Fine Arts, Boston

MFA PUBLICATIONS
a division of the Museum of Fine Arts, Boston
465 Huntington Avenue
Boston, Massachusetts 02115
www.mfa-publications.org

For a complete listing of MFA Publications, please contact the publisher at the above address, or call 617 369 3438.

The cover motif, as well as the watercolor ornaments used on the title page and contents page and in the "Album" section, were adapted from a photographic album produced by the Adolfo Farsari studio, now in the Jean S. and Frederic A. Sharf Collection at the Museum of Fine Arts, Boston.

ISBN 0-87846-683-5 (slipcased hardcover)
ISBN 0-87846-682-7 (softcover)
Library of Congress Control Number: 2004100392

Edited by Emiko K. Usui and Mark Polizzotti
Designed by Mark Polizzotti

Available to the trade through:
D.A.P. / Distributed Art Publishers
155 Sixth Avenue, 2nd floor
New York, New York 10013
Tel.: 212 627 1999 · Fax: 212 627 9484

FIRST EDITION
Printed on acid-free paper
Printed and bound in Italy

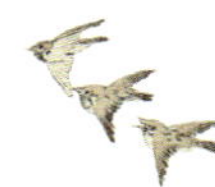

Contents

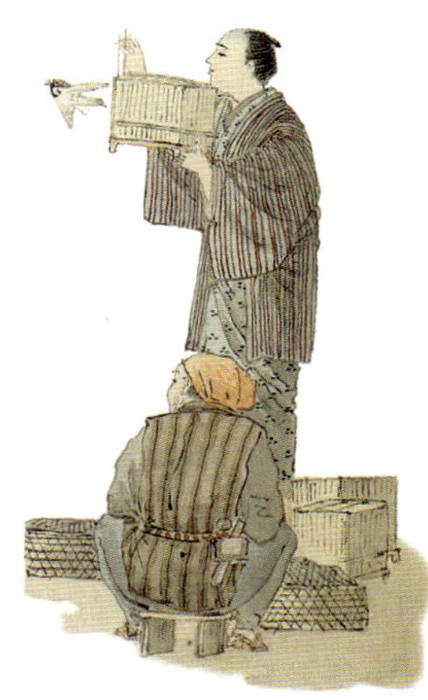

A Traveler's Paradise

FREDERIC A. SHARF

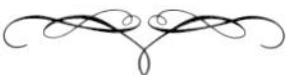

FROM THE VERY BEGINNINGS OF THE MEIJI ERA (1868–1912), Westerners came to Japan. Some were employed by the Meiji government as advisers to assist its efforts in modernizing the country; others came as official diplomatic representatives; still others as Christian missionaries; and a handful of men came to pursue business opportunities. Finally, Japan increasingly became a destination for an elite group of wealthy, sophisticated, adventurous tourists, who have left behind precious descriptions of their travels and of Japanese life as they encountered it.

At first, travel to Japan was not easy. Two events in 1869 began to change that, however: in May, transcontinental rail travel across the United States became a reality; and in November, the opening of the Suez Canal created a shortcut from Europe to Asia. From 1870 to 1900, the greater ease of access created a new industry within Japan — the tourist industry — and the gradual increase in arriving travelers led to a rapid growth in demand for high-quality photographs. A new profession was born to document people and places, creating in the process a unique record of Meiji Japan.

The first scheduled trans-Pacific steamship service from San Francisco to Hong Kong (via Yokohama, Kobe, and Nagasaki) was initiated by the Pacific Mail Steamship Company in 1867. Four wooden-hulled, paddlewheel steamships made the trip from San Francisco to Yokohama in twenty-four days. Retired American Secretary of State William H. Seward, accompanied by Olive, his adopted daughter, embarked on September 1, 1870. She described their voyage as follows:

> The vessels of the Pacific Mail Line are side-wheel steamers, and in accommodations and appointments are surpassed only by the palatial boats on the Hudson River and Long Island Sound. The "China," four thousand tons burden, is the smallest of them all. We enjoy an uninterrupted promenade seven hundred feet in circuit on the upper deck. We have sixty cabin class passengers and might carry comfortably twice that number . . . The gentlemen amuse themselves with gymnastic games, the ladies with music and books. An expert Japanese juggler entertains us in the cabin. In steerage are five hundred Chinese returning home . . .

In 1874, the Union Pacific and Central Pacific Railways created its own line, the Occidental and Oriental Steamship Company, in order to provide seamless service from the East Coast of the United States to the seaports of Asia. The resulting competition between the two steamship lines led to the replacement of the outdated sidewheelers by iron-hulled, screw-propelled steamships. Travel across the Pacific had become quicker (dropping to below twenty days) and more comfortable. By the mid-1880s, a Bostonian could reach San Francisco in seven days by train and, allowing for a brief layover there, would reach Yokohama in less than four weeks.

The concept of global travel was popularized by the publication in 1872 of Jules Verne's classic novel, *Around the World in Eighty Days*. Verne established a hypothetical standard when he developed the itinerary for his character Phineas Fogg: forty-two days from London to Yokohama; twenty-nine days from Yokohama to New York; and the remaining nine days from New York back to London. (Europeans could in fact reach Yokohama in forty-two days from London by taking the Peninsular and Orient [P & O] Steamships, and in even less time from Marseille on the steamships of the Messageries Maritimes Steamship Line.)

During the 1880s, the New York publisher Joseph Pulitzer decided to test Verne's hypothesis, and in the fall of 1889 an enterprising female reporter named Nellie Bly convinced his newspaper, the *New York World*, to sponsor her attempt. When the proprietors of the rival *Cosmopolitan Magazine* heard about it, they assigned their own reporter, Elizabeth Bisland, to attempt the same journey, but in the opposite direction.

On November 14, 1889, Bly departed New York City heading east for London and on to Asia via the Suez Canal route. She made remarkable connections along the way and on January 25, after seventy-two days, she was back in New York City, where she was lionized by the American media. Meanwhile, Bisland had left New York City on the same day, traveling by train to San Francisco (she crossed the United States in less than five days). Her good luck ran out on the final leg of her journey, when she ran into bad weather on the North Atlantic and lost the race, eventually reaching New York on January 29, after seventy-six days. Both women had beaten the Jules Verne standard; their journeys highlighted both the potential of travel and the vagaries of such factors as weather.

Ironically, in the decade that followed, the completion of the Canadian Pacific Railway across Canada, and the construction of three state-of-the-art steamships for their subsidiary the Canadian Pacific Steamship Company, made the Canadian route the quickest way to Yokohama. By the end of the century, a Bostonian could reach Yokohama in three weeks, while an enterprising Londoner could do it in four, if all connections went smoothly.

* * * * *

At Yokohama, steamships anchored in a large natural harbor crowded with a vast array of ships (merchant sailing ships, steamships, and warships of many nations); there was no breakwater and no pier on which to unload. Passengers and cargo disembarked onto small steam launches and Japanese sampans for the short (but often very turbulent) ride to the Bund, a wide waterfront street facing the harbor.

On arrival, the traveler was struck by, in the words of Bostonian Harry Hughes, "a most curious mixture of East and West." Jinrikisha pullers, often scantily dressed, were visitors' first contacts with Japan (and, not surprisingly, the subject of numerous photographs); Western buildings lined the opposite side of the Bund, "the only decently wide street" in Yokohama. The initial destination was a hotel, of which the Grand Hotel, opened in 1873, was the most frequented.

Yokohama was divided into three distinct sections. Looking

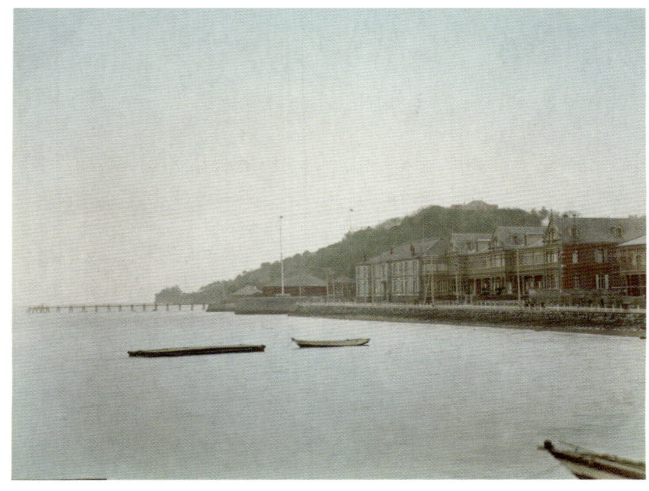

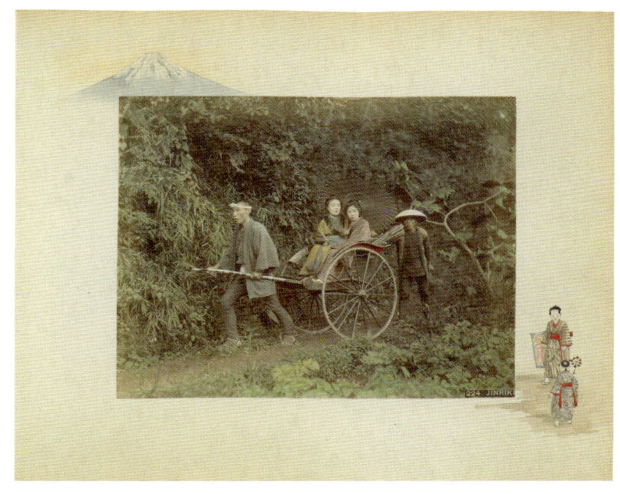

A traveler's first views of Yokohama: the Bund (left) as seen from the harbor, and a page from an album (right) showing a jinrikisha puller and passengers

inward from the harbor there was a hill on the left, known as the Bluff, where Westerners lived in Western-style houses, surrounded by Western hospitals and schools. The central area that faced the harbor at sea level was known as the Settlement, the location of Western businesses and hotels. The entire right side of the cityscape was known as the Japanese Town, the location of Japanese shops and homes. Japanese Town included three famous streets: Honchō-dōri (Main Street), where the elegant shops were located; Benten-dōri (also known as Curio Street), with popular-priced souvenir and gift shops; and Isezaki-chō (or Theatre Street), which housed low-priced bazaars as well as places in which traditional Japanese food and entertainment could be enjoyed.

Gradually, between 1872 and 1900, Yokohama was transformed into a city with a decidedly Western appearance: streets were paved with macadam and lit by gaslight; sidewalks were installed; a municipal waterworks was opened in 1887; a proper pier was completed in the harbor in 1894, and a breakwater in 1896. By the 1890s, the city was defined architecturally by important buildings, constructed of red brick trimmed with granite — a style that became associated with all important cities in Meiji Japan.

* * * * *

The word "travel" is an English adaptation of the French word *travail*, meaning "work"; thus, by definition, a nineteenth-century traveler was expected to work at the experience, and to do so properly required detailed, informative guidebooks.

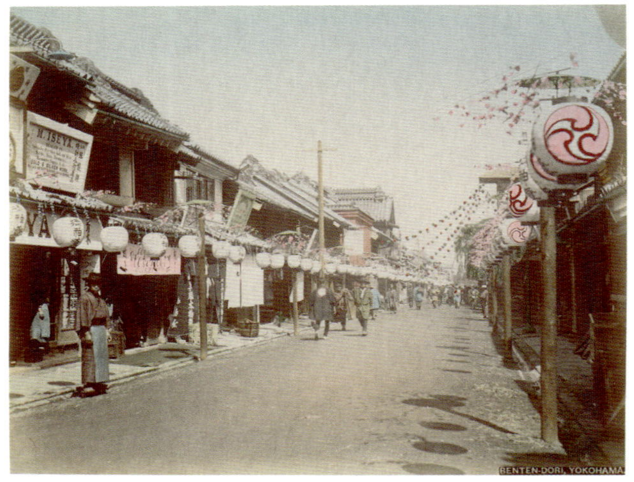

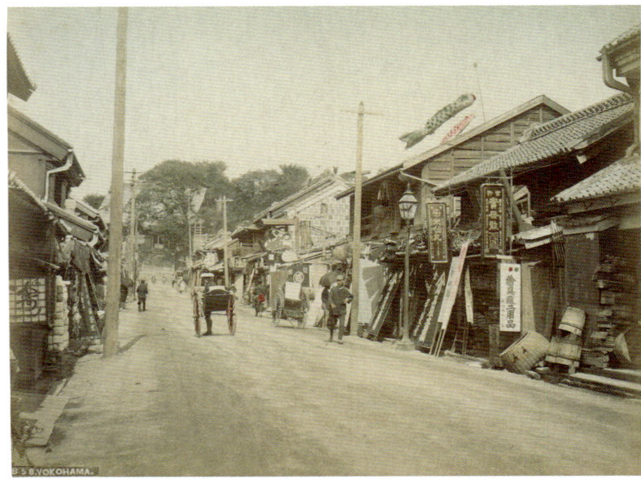

Two views of Yokohama: Benten-dōri by Tamamura Kōzaburō and Motomachi Nichōme by an unknown photographer

While travelers to Japan in the years before 1880 were accustomed to relying on prior travelers' accounts, including the experience of Commodore Perry in 1854, the development of organized, scheduled access to Japan during the 1870s pointed to the need for better guidebooks. Adolfo Farsari, an Italian-born, Yokohama-based entrepreneur, was among the most prolific publishers of documentary materials to assist the traveler.

He began by producing a series of maps in 1878, featuring both English and Japanese identification of important places easily reached from Yokohama. By July 1880, Farsari produced his first official guidebook to Japan (*Tourists' Guide to Yokohama, Tokio, Hakone, Fujiyama, Kamakura, Yokosuka, Kanozan, Narita, Nikko, Kioto, Osaka Etc. Etc.*). The book was famous for its brevity and aimed at travelers with limited time for exploration.

The market, however, was ripe for an extensive, authoritative publication, in the portable format that had been made popular by the German publisher Baedecker and the British publisher Murray. Such a book was published in February 1881 in a small edition of five hundred copies and in a format that copied Murray's "Handbook" series: *A Handbook for Travellers in Central and Northern Japan*. The compilers, Ernest M. Satow and A. G. S. Hawes, provided the traveler with 489 pages — in contrast to Farsari's 92 pages — of historical notes, extensive descriptions of important sights, suggested itineraries that varied with the amount of time a traveler could spend, and practical details that could facilitate travel anywhere in Japan.

A new edition in 1884 was called *Murray's Handbook for Travelers in Japan*. While John Murray in London allowed the authors to give their publication official status as part of his extensive range, he was not willing to actually use his own money to produce this edition — a clear indication of how small the tourist market to Japan was at this time. The authors paid for the printing of one thousand copies of the 1884 edition, recovering their costs from the sales. By 1891, however, Murray was confident enough to produce a third edition at his own risk. Rapid changes taking place within Japan (most noticeably the increase in railroad access), combined with steady growth in tourism, caused Murray to publish new editions regularly from 1894 to 1913.

The language of *Murray's Handbook Japan* rapidly became the verbal lens through which a traveler interpreted the country's sights. The guidebooks told the visitor exactly what he was expected to see and exactly what each sight meant. The message of the guidebook was reinforced by the presence of licensed guides (an association of English-speaking licensed guides had existed in Yokohama since 1878). Most serious travelers retained such a person as soon as they arrived in Yokohama, and often the guide remained with his customer for the latter's entire stay in Japan.

While the guidebooks described Japan, it was the photographs that conveyed the exotic, colorful, scenic appearance that so enthralled the first generation of travelers. The growth of printed descriptions of Japan could not keep pace with the growth of photographic depictions. The importance of such images is reflected in the diaries of every traveler who recorded his or her reminiscences.

It was not uncommon for an arriving traveler to immediately visit a photographic studio, buying photos of places he had not yet seen. The New York doctor Albert Leffingwell landed in Yokohama in July 1881. After checking in at the Grand Hotel, he went at once to a bookseller and a photographer:

> Photographs are always of interest, and are surprisingly cheap — a penny each. As my purchase seems likely to be considerable for him, he determines to treat, and sending out a servant, she returns with two glasses of iced-water to our better acquaintance.

While the traveler wanted to acquire photos of Japan, he also wanted to have his own photo taken, and the studios in Yokohama (and elsewhere in Japan) began to provide an assortment of Japanese props, including complete Japanese outfits, in order to satisfy their Western customers. A Philadelphian, Charles M. Taylor, Jr., described his 1896 visit to the studio of Kusakabe Kimbei*:

> Mr. Kimbei [*sic*], whose studio is situated upon Honcho-dori Street is the best photographer in Yokohama. We enter with our guide, and upon making known our wishes are shown upstairs to a dressing-room, where a charming little Japanese girl dresses the foreign ladies in Japanese costume. A Japanese gentleman is also engaged to attire the men. This assistance is quite necessary. When dressed, we are told to sit Japanese fashion, that is, to cross the legs under one; and we remain in this uncomfortable position until our photographs are taken.

Photographic studios also provided the traveler with an assortment of albums into which the photos could be mounted. Albums were available with lacquer covers on which Japanese

* *All Japanese names appear in traditional style, with surnames before given names.*

scenes were depicted, or with sophisticated woven silk fabric covers. Albums could be assembled with accordion leaves, so that a number of images could be displayed at one time, or in traditional Western format. Most albums contained prints in 8 by 10–inch format, but they were also available with 3½ by 5½–inch prints. All photos were hand-colored.

* * * * *

Travelers seeking to move around Japan prior to 1899 had to obtain an internal passport. When Japan was opened to foreign visitors, the Japanese government gave Westerners access to five Treaty Ports (Yokohama, Kobe, Nagasaki, Hakodate, and Niigate) and two Open Cities (Tokyo and Osaka). In order to travel twenty-five miles outside any of these seven cities, an internal passport was required; such documents defined in English and Japanese certain rules that must be followed while outside the limits of the seven cities.

Passports were easy to obtain, normally requiring twenty-four hours for a Yokohama traveler (the passports were issued in Tokyo). The various Western consulates in Yokohama organized the documentation. Prior to 1894, a traveler would need to state his intended internal destination; from 1894 to 1899, no details were required, as Japan became more comfortable with Western visitors. In 1899, the entire passport system was abolished.

Having obtained a passport, travelers were in a position to explore Japan. Ease of internal access was one goal of Meiji government policy. In 1869, a Department of Public Works was established with a mandate to construct railroad lines. The first line (eighteen miles in length) connected Yokohama with Tokyo; Emperor Meiji presided over the opening ceremonies on October 12, 1872. Kobe

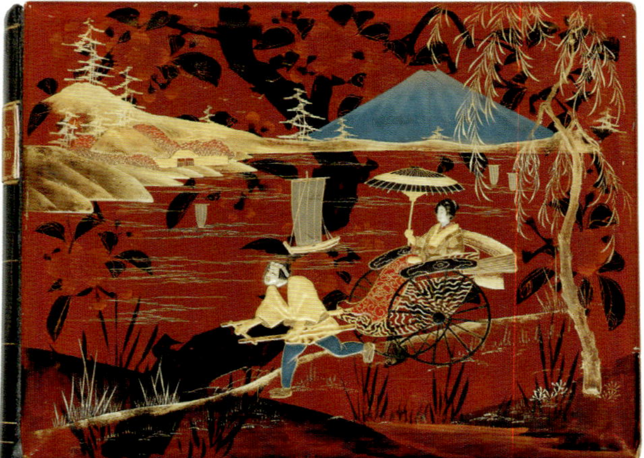

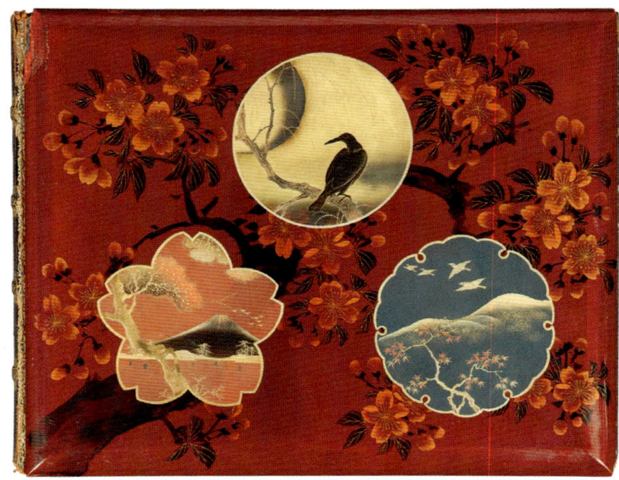

Lacquer photograph album covers, from an unidentified Yokohama studio (top) and the studio of Adolfo Farsari (bottom)

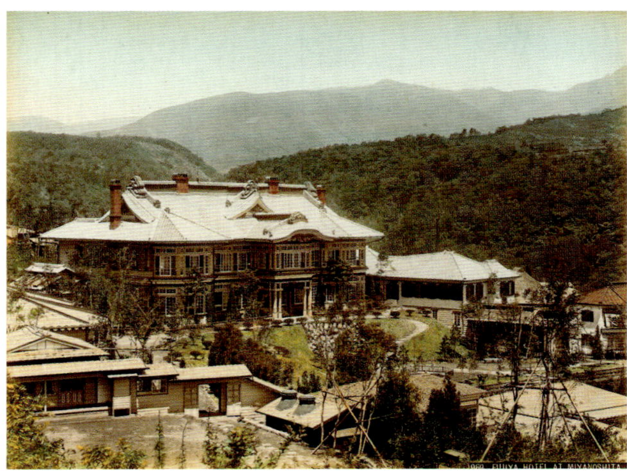

The Fujiya Hotel in Miyanoshita (about 1891) by Kusakabe Kimbei

was connected to Osaka in 1874, and to Kyoto in 1876, and ultimately with Tokyo in 1889. Two years later, train service was available from Tokyo north to Aomori. By the turn of the century, a traveler could reach most important attractions by train.

As access to and within Japan improved during the last thirty years of the nineteenth century, there was a concomitant need to create hotels. The very earliest accommodations in Yokohama were geisha houses, whose Japanese proprietors learned to cater to Western tastes in food and decoration.

The first Western-style hotel in Japan opened in Tokyo in 1868 — a handsome two-story brick building with views of Tokyo Bay located at Tsukiji (with 102 bedrooms, a dining room, and a billiard room). It was unsuccessful in attracting guests, and when it was destroyed by fire in April 1872 it was never rebuilt. The capital city did not have a first-class Western hotel until November 1890, when the Imperial Hotel opened — interestingly with only sixty guest bedrooms, of which ten were suites earmarked for dignitaries.

Most travelers preferred to stay in Yokohama, where there were two important hotels — the Grand Hotel, opened in 1873 and overlooking the harbor; and the smaller Club Hotel. Guest room capacity was limited: in 1899, the Club Hotel had only twenty-five rooms, and the Grand Hotel finally expanded to one hundred guest rooms in 1900. This minuscule capacity provides us with some feeling for the small size of the tourist market in this period.

Important hotels developed in places frequented by travelers: Miyanoshita (Mount Fuji), Nikkō, Kyoto, Kobe, and Nagasaki. The development of the famous Fujiya Hotel in Miyanoshita provides an interesting insight into the process by which Japanese entrepreneurs created a hotel industry that could attract Western visitors.

Yamaguchi Sennosuke, the man behind the Fujiya Hotel, came from a family of geisha-house operators. Their Yokohama establishment, widely known as "Nectarine" or "No. 9," was world-famous among sailors and prominent in the portfolios of the Yokohama photo studios. With family backing, Yamaguchi purchased an old inn in Miyanoshita, renovated it for Western tastes, and opened for business in July 1878.

Yamaguchi not only provided his guests with "good foreign beds," "wines and liquors at reasonable prices," and the "luxury of ice" on hot summer days, he also convinced the young Yokohama photographer Shima Shūkichi to establish a studio on land adjacent to the hotel entrance. Shima prospered, providing views of the Hakone region to the Yokohama studios and to the Fujiya guests.

His wife and daughter hand-colored his photos and ultimately extended the same service to photos taken by guests at the Fujiya.

Yamaguchi used the photos taken by Shima to promote his hotel; advertisements for the Fujiya Hotel always made reference to the presence of Shima. When the Tōkaidō Railway line (service from Tokyo to Kobe) was completed in 1889, access to Miyanoshita was considerably easier and made more so by Yamaguchi building his own road to take travelers the last few miles up a steep, rocky hill from Yumoto.

Yamaguchi continued to improve his property: he added an electrical power-generating facility in 1893, built a home on his property for the famous scholar and author Basil Hall Chamberlain (who had taken over the job of creating updated text for the *Murray's Handbook Japan*), and sold some of his land to Emperor Meiji on which to build an imperial summer home.

By 1900, there was a network of established hotels in all important cities frequented by travelers, with accommodation and food known to be acceptable for Westerners. Although not yet in its heyday, travel in Japan was already a well-organized business.

* * * * *

Travelers to Japan at the turn of the century were voracious consumers of photographs, but their presence alone does not account for the country's enormous photographic output at that time. Two other factors contributed to the dynamic growth of this business.

First, there was a substantial export market. Photographs and albums were stocked by dealers in Western cities, and presumably purchased by people who never set foot in Japan itself. Second, there was an even larger "floating" market, composed of merchant seamen whose visits to Japan were confined to major seaports where cargo was unloaded, as well as sailors on the warships maintained in Asia (on the so-called China Station) by all Western powers, who regularly visited Yokohama, Kobe, and Nagasaki, often for stays of many weeks.

In 1895, the major powers (England, United States, France, Germany, and Russia) had more than forty warships between them that regularly visited Japan — resulting in many thousands of visitors who bought albums for their own amusement or to send home to their families. In 1898, the United States established a presence in the Philippines, and over the next four years more than sixty thousand American soldiers were sent out, all of whom stopped in Japan (normally Nagasaki) in order for their ships to refuel.

There is probably no accurate record as to how many photographs would have been produced from 1870 through 1900, but the evidence of substantial production exists in libraries and collections all over the Western world. The fact that so many photos were sold to people who never visited Japan, or whose visit was brief, accounts for the nature of the subject matter. Commercial photographers produced images for a market whose preconception of Japan was established by written descriptions of the people and the places. In the final account, Japan was a traveler's paradise not only for its increasing number of visitors, but even — and largely on the strength of images such as are contained in this book — for many people who never actually went there.

Yokohama Shashin

SEBASTIAN DOBSON

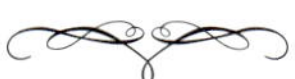

YOKOHAMA SHASHIN, literally, "Yokohama photographs," were named after the bustling coastal town that was both the center of their production and the primary port of entry for foreigners coming to Japan during the Meiji era. The vibrant, hand-colored images enjoyed enormous popularity among international visitors, serving them as souvenirs of famous sights, traditional costumes, and aspects of Japanese daily life that were quickly disappearing in the wake of modernization. At their best, Yokohama *shashin* represented a unique fusion of Western photographic technology and traditional Japanese craftsmanship: sepia monochrome prints were painstakingly hand-colored by artists and then mounted on album leaves, often also decorated by hand, and bound in albums with silk brocade covers or lacquer boards inlaid with ivory, mother-of-pearl, and gold.

Because the images were aimed to appeal to foreign taste, and even staged or composed artificially in order to do so, they have been perceived by some as pandering to nineteenth-century Western notions of exoticism. This conclusion has sometimes caused the whole genre to be dismissed as nothing more than tourist kitsch, despite the care with which the best of the photographs were created. The condemnation is unfair, for it is precisely because these studies were constructed for a particular clientele that the images remain a valuable visual record of Japan at the time. Three photographers in particular — Adolfo Farsari, Kusakabe Kimbei, and Tamamura Kōzaburō — enjoyed great success during the 1880s and 1890s as exponents of Yokohama *shashin*, and each of their careers offers a different perspective on the genre. Before describing these, however, it is necessary to examine the history of photography in Japan before their arrival.

JAPAN'S EARLY PHOTOGRAPHIC INDUSTRY

In terms of numbers, the center of Japan's early photographic industry was not Yokohama. At the beginning of the Meiji era, in 1867, for example, it was reported to the British Foreign Office that in "Asaka [Osaka], a Japanese town of 30,000 inhabitants in which trade is very active," there were no fewer than forty native photographers "kept busy at their profession,"[1] while in Yokohama in 1869 there were no more than four commercial photographers at work, of whom one was non-Japanese.[2] During the 1860s and 1870s, Tokyo had the strongest claim as the center of the Japanese photographic trade, and three of the most successful Japanese photographers to practice in Yokohama in the late 1860s, Shimooka Renjō, Uchida Kuichi, and Shimizu Tōkoku, even relocated to the capital. At that time, the enterprising photographer served two different, but not necessarily mutually exclusive, client bases. The most common were those clients — either Japanese or foreign — who simply required their likenesses to be taken, and many studios appear to have thrived by catering solely to this steady demand for photographic portraits. The other and more lucrative clientele — almost exclusively foreign — sought photographs that depicted the scenery of Japan and the "manners and customs" of its inhabitants. These early souvenir buyers came from a diverse community of foreign residents in Yokohama, whether diplomats, missionaries, merchants, or members of the Western military garrisons and naval squadrons assigned to the treaty ports at that time for their protection.

In the early 1870s, a new kind of visitor — the foreign tourist — started coming to Japan. Taking advantage of recent advances in worldwide transportation links and a new era of relative security, travelers making the journey more for pleasure than business descended on all the treaty ports, and Yokohama in particular. As Frederic Sharf shows in the previous essay, the arrival of such tourists had an enormous impact on the Yokohama economy, prompting the creation of new, Western-style hotels, the publication of English-language maps and guidebooks, and the development of new industries producing goods and services aimed at the short-term visitor. The local photographic industry was no exception.

The shift from a resident to a tourist market had a profound effect on how photographers in Yokohama created and marketed their portfolios of photographs. Whereas most foreign residents had acquired their knowledge of Japan through long-term acquaintance with their adopted country, the average globetrotter had only a short time in which to do so, and, furnished with a guidebook, already came with ideas about the preindustrial idyll that was presumed to lie beyond the treaty ports. Taking their cues from the itineraries recommended in these guidebooks, some photographers included in their portfolio views of such well-known places and neatly packaged them in albums of fifty or one hundred photographs. For the less enterprising traveler, purchasing one of these albums could even act as a substitute for the experience of traveling itself.

THE BEGINNING OF PHOTOGRAPHY IN YOKOHAMA

Although commercial photographers were active in Yokohama from 1860, the first to appreciate the potential of selling photographs in albums was the British photographer Felice Beato (born 1833 or 1834), who arrived in Yokohama in the summer of 1863.[3] Within a short time, Beato standardized the format, and a price list printed between 1864 and 1865 indicates that he offered his clients "complete albums" of one hundred photographs or "half albums" of fifty. Despite the setback of losing much of his stock in a fire in 1866, by 1868 Beato was able to introduce his work in elegant Western-style, leather-bound albums, with photographs mounted on the recto side of each leaf and a printed label bearing an accompanying description pasted on the page opposite. For clients who could afford it, Beato offered his best albums as two-volume collections, consisting of one hundred hand-tinted portraits and studies of "native types" and one hundred untinted landscape works.[4] Beato was also astute enough, however, to create packages for every pocket. In the *Japan Punch*, Charles Wirgman published a witty caricature of his friend's "Album Thermometer," satirizing in what purported to be direct quotations from Beato his various reactions to clients depending on the quantity of photographs in each album they bought from him.

The commercial success of Beato's albums quickly inspired imitators in Yokohama's then-small community of photographers, and among his first impressions of the port when he arrived there in 1870, the American William Griffis noted that "photographic establishments tempt our eye and purse with tasteful albums of Japanese costume and scenery."[5] Given that Beato was the only foreign photographer issuing albums at that time, it would appear that at least a couple of his Japanese competitors were following suit, but no examples of their work in this format have yet been identified.

Starting in 1871, another foreign photographer, the Austrian Baron Raimund von Stillfried-Ratenicz (1839–1911), is known to have used the same album format to market a portfolio that consisted predominantly of landscapes, under the general title of "Views and Costumes of Japan." Stillfried, however, in a departure from Beato's practice, dispensed with printed explanatory labels altogether and instead placed brief captions in the negatives of his landscape photographs. By 1876, he was producing albums that, like Beato's, separated his portfolio evenly into "Costumes" and "Views" and, as the scholar Luke Gartlan has shown, phased out the captions in the negatives of his landscapes through various processes until he had produced "a generic portfolio of scenes unhindered by textual direction."[6] Stillfried and his business partner Hermann Andersen pursued this genre with such success that in 1877 they bought out Beato's studio and merged the two studios' portfolios into one under the name of the Japan Photographic Association.

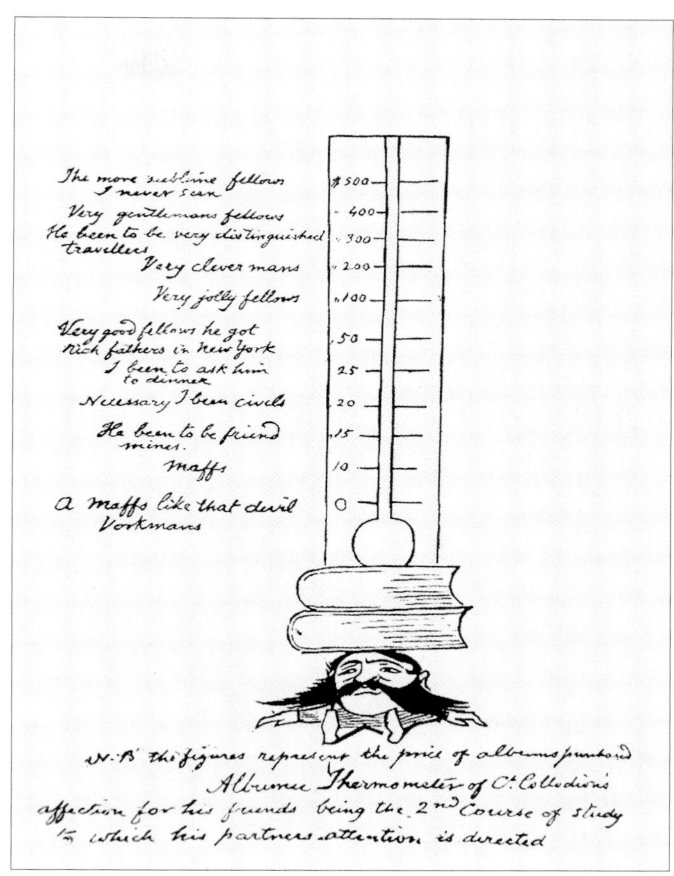

The Beato "Album Thermometer," from Japan Punch

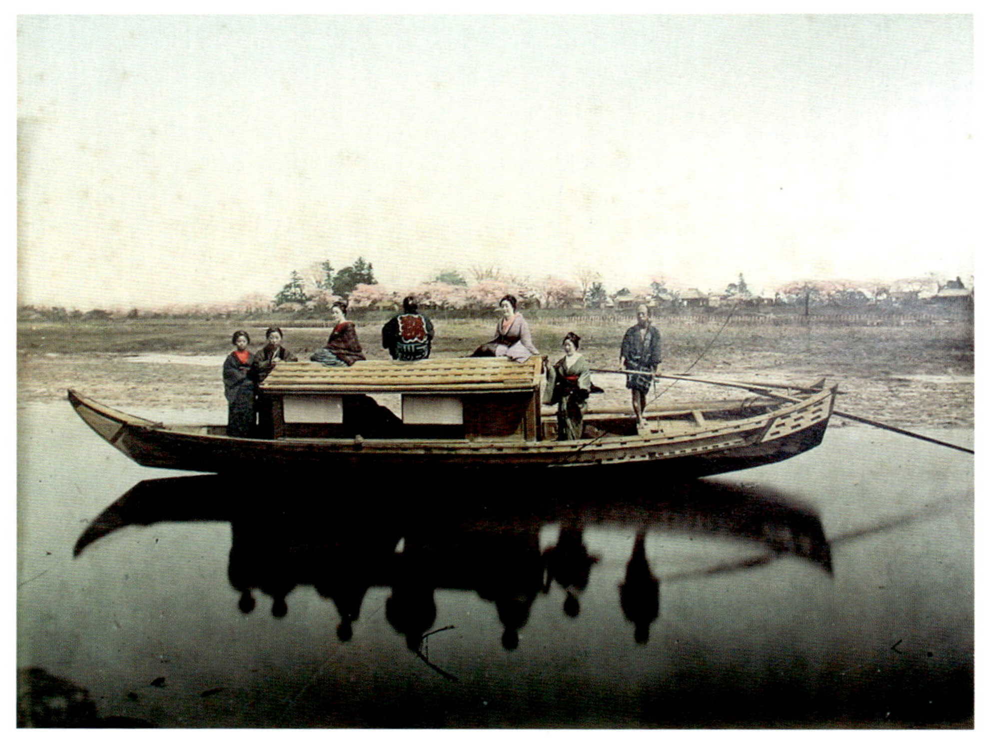

One of Uchida Kuichi's "very excellent views": Pleasure boat on the Sumida River near Mukōjima

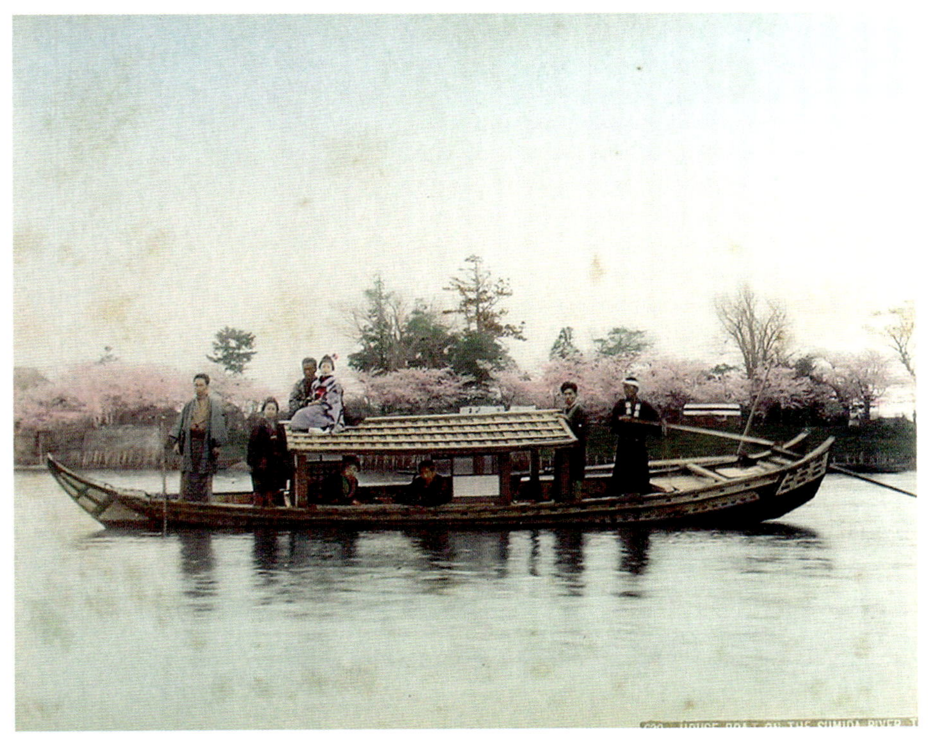

The same scene as reimagined by Kusakabe Kimbei

One of the earliest extant albums by a Japanese photographer dates from 1872. It consists of fifty-seven photographs taken by Uchida Kuichi of places visited by Emperor Meiji during his first imperial tour of western Japan. Lavishly bound in two traditional Japanese *orihon* or "accordion" albums, each decorated with brocade covers and endpapers flecked with silver gilt, the photographs are accompanied by handwritten paper labels in Japanese pasted in each mount.[7] Uchida was the first Japanese photographer whose portfolio received attention — and hence publicity — in the English-language press. In a note to his readers of May 1873, the editor of the *Far East* presented "some very excellent views taken by Mr. Uchida, a Japanese photographer of singular ability" and recommended his studio in Asakusa as well worth a visit. If Uchida deliberately sought foreign custom, he did so with discretion, maintaining not only the decorum one would expect of a photographer enjoying the favor of the Imperial household but also a strong sense of his own value. One rare foreign visitor to leave a record of his visit to Uchida's studio in Asakusa was Henry Smith Munro, an American employee of the Japanese government, who reported in 1874 in a letter home:

> the photographer here who takes the best landscapes is Uchida — a Japanese — I have looked over his magnificent collection of 50 pictures!! — and want to buy them all — but the price is $250.00 — "50 cents for one picture, $250 for 50 — I have but one price." The execution is perfect — and the landscape subjects are admirably well chosen — real artistic pictures!![8]

Few other early Japanese photographers were recorded in their own words so memorably, and Uchida's pronouncement, "I have but one price," indicates a confidence in his ability, which, although justified, much have struck foreign visitors to his studio as remarkable, especially at a time when most Japanese photographers were attempting to undercut their rivals' prices. For young Munro, Uchida's portfolio cost three-quarters of the monthly salary he received as an otherwise well-paid foreign adviser.

The year 1881 proved remarkable for photography in Yokohama. Almost as if to make up for lost time, eight new Japanese-owned studios were established in the treaty port, including that of Kusakabe Kimbei. Even with the increased opportunities offered by tourism, this initial flurry of activity was more than the local economy could sustain at that time, and within the year, six of them had disappeared. A new trend had emerged, however, and for an ambitious young photographer such as Tamamura Kōzaburō it was apparent that Asakusa was no longer the place to be, and he duly relocated his studio to Yokohama in 1882.

Foreign-owned studios, by contrast, went into decline. Felice Beato, who had so long dominated the photographic scene before the Meiji Restoration, left Japan for good in 1884 after selling his studio to Baron von Stillfried in 1877; von Stillfried, likewise, quit Japan in 1881, leaving his younger brother, Franz, to operate a photographic studio under the family name and title in Yokohama, until he also sold in 1883 and left Japan two years later to move to America. The Yokohama Photographic Company, owned by the elder Baron von Stillfried's former business partner and recent rival, Hermann Andersen, did not long outlast the Stillfried brothers and was soon bought out by Adolfo Farsari in 1885. By the end of 1886, only Farsari and the Chinese photographer Tong Cheong were still in business, and one year later, Farsari was the only foreign photographer operating in Yokohama, and indeed in Japan.

Adolfo Farsari (1841–1898) is first listed as a resident in Yokohama in 1873. His business, Sargent, Farsari and Company, located at Number 80 on Honchō-dōri, offered its clients, "Guide Books and Maps of Japan, Japanese and English Conversation Books and Dictionaries, Photographic Views of All Parts of the Empire, Latest Newspapers, Magazines and Novels by every Mail . . . [and] Smokers' Supplies of every Description," in addition to printing stationery and visiting cards.[9] It is not clear who was responsible for the photographic views, and the division of labor between the partners is likewise unclear. Farsari's most readily identifiable contribution to the company's stock was cartographic — he is recorded producing maps of Miyanoshita and Yokohama and its environs — but it is evident that the publishing side of the operation also interested him. After breaking up with Sargent, Farsari and Company came to publish all future editions of *Keeling's Guide to Japan*, and Farsari himself later wrote and published a phrase book, *Japanese Words and Phrases for the Use of Strangers*.

It was probably as a result of his involvement in the tourist trade that Farsari became aware of the commercial opportunities of photography, for his company brought him into contact with the same client base that would later buy his photo albums. As he wrote to his sister, he approached photography in a businesslike fashion. He felt that "taking pictures is just a mechanical thing," and he was essentially self-taught: "I have had no real teachers, I have learned everything from books. I bought all the necessary equipment and with no help from anyone, I printed, took photographs and so on. Then I taught others."[10] The first step, however, was to take over an existing photographic studio. In 1885, there were two foreign-owned studios operating in the Yokohama foreign settlement, the Japan Photographic Association and the similar-sounding Yokohama Photographic Company, which were located next door to each other on the Bund. In February of that year, Farsari entered into a partnership with Tamamura Kōzaburō in order to acquire the Japan Photographic Association.[11] Farsari's acquisition gave him not only an existing portfolio, which included the work of Felice Beato and Baron von Stillfried, but also considerable cachet, and he seemed content for a while to use the existing album title page of his predecessors with a discreet overstamp applied in the lower margin.

The arrival of the new occupant of Number 17 augured a change in the photographic trade. A caricature in the February 1885 issue of the *Japan Punch* showed the owner of the Yokohama Photographic Company studio next door, David Welsh, in a bluff, stage-Irishman guise already familiar to the journal's readers, scoffing at the competition offered by Farsari's studio — "Farce it is, begorra!!" — while the editor's comment, "No. 16 is excoited, ha! ha!," hinted at his unease. *Punch*-san was prescient: the Yokohama Photographic Company soon disappeared from the scene, and within the year, Farsari had moved his studio into Welsh's former premises.

Business was brisk, to the extent that Farsari would later complain that if a fire had not destroyed his studio and stock in February 1886, he would have been able to retire after four years. Farsari certainly suffered heavy losses as a result of the fire, but it did have the positive effect of obliging him to create a completely new portfolio of photographs. The rest of the year was spent assembling this portfolio. For at least five months, Farsari toured across Japan, photographing the main tourist attractions along the

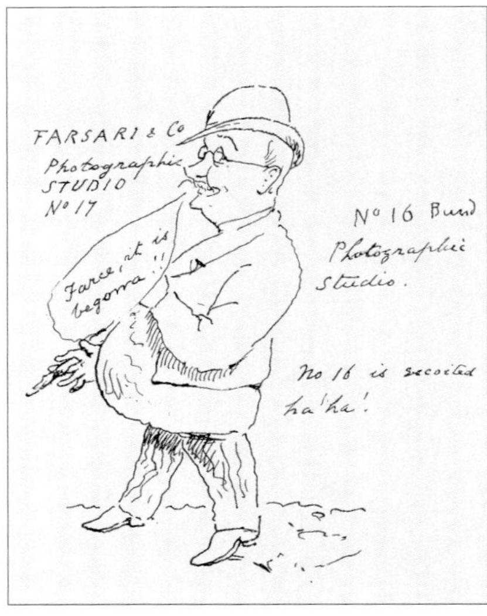

A caricature in Japan Punch *heralding the rise of Farsari's studio*

celebrated roads of Edo-period Japan. Several more months were spent "straightening things up," and presumably creating a portfolio of genre portraits, before Farsari could finally reopen his studio at the beginning of 1887. By 1889, Farsari's stock consisted of approximately one thousand negatives of Japanese landscapes and "types."

The new studio proved an even greater success, and the new portfolio received a glowing review in the *Photographic Times and American Photographer*, to which Farsari had sent a collection of colored photographs "that excite our admiration. Not only are they technically almost perfect, but also the selection of the subjects shows much artistic proportion. They depict Japanese life in various phases, and also something of the natural beauty of this picturesque land, so little known in our country."[12] Farsari was so proud of this encomium that he reprinted it in an advertisement for his studio, italicizing the reference to "artistic proportion." A later visitor to the Farsari studio, the author and globetrotter Rudyard Kipling, waxed lyrical about the photographs, telling his readers in India,

> if you buy nothing else in Japan, and you will break yourself unless you begin as a pauper, you must buy photographs, and the best are to be found at the house of Farsari and Co. whose reputation extends from Saigon even to America. Mr. Farsari is a nice man, eccentric and an artist, for which peculiarities he makes you pay, but his wares are worth the money . . . Seriously, spend as much money as you can on Farsari and let him choose the illustrations of Japanese.[13]

Although Farsari took considerable pride in being the only European photographer in Japan, he was intelligent enough to realize that given the number of Japanese competitors in Yokohama — "so numerous," he remarked, "that one cannot throw a stone up in the air without hitting a photographer" — this was not enough. Quality was Farsari's selling point, and at a time when most Japanese photographers were seeking to undercut one another, he refused to compromise on quality and priced his work accordingly. In an advertisement announcing the reopening of his studio in 1887, Farsari explained to would-be clients: "As we are sure that, when our photographs have been compared with others, one will not purchase elsewhere, we respectfully request that every studio in Yokohama be visited by intending purchasers before making a selection. Our pictures may be more expensive than others, but as we use the best materials and our painting is so far superior that it cannot even be compared with similar productions in Japan, the elegance of the work will well repay the extra outlay." Farsari even posted a notice at the entrance to his studio advising visitors that if they were unable to appreciate why his photographs were more expensive than those at other studios, they should take their business elsewhere.

The attention paid to coloring positioned the photographs of the Farsari studio above the competition, and this quality was featured in his advertising: "the colors were carefully noted at the time that the photographs of temples and other structures were taken, and we are the only ones who paint them as they really are." Kipling bore out this claim during his visit to Yokohama in 1889 by observing, "a colored photograph ought to be an abomination. It generally is, but Farsari knows how to color accurately and according to the scale of lights in this fantastic country. On the deck of the steamer I laughed at his red and blue hillsides. In the hills I saw he has painted true."[14]

This endeavor required a team of colorists, and a survey of 1891 indicates that out of a total of thirty-two employees at Farsari and Company, nineteen were "painters." The influential William K. Burton, a professor at Tokyo Imperial University and the author of the popular *A.B.C. of Photography*, visited Farsari's studio in 1887 and saw the colorists at work:

> In the Gallery of A. Farsari and Co. I had the pleasure of seeing the native artists at work. They were to be seen busily engaged in a large room, each artist in the position almost universally adopted by a Japanese for his work, namely squatting on a straw mat . . . Farsari's artists were very slow and careful in their work. He informed me that he was satisfied if each colored two or three prints in a day. This allows time enough for each print to be really well colored, and indeed I have seen no better work in the way of colored photographs anywhere than some of Farsari's productions.[15]

Farsari's method involved rigorous — and, for the first few months, unpaid — instruction, with Farsari himself interviewing each potential colorist to establish whether he was familiar with Japanese painting techniques, then training the successful applicant, eventually giving him a basic salary, and then steadily increasing it until Farsari was completely satisfied with the quality of his work. For the capable and loyal employee, the rewards were good: a colorist at the Farsari studio could earn twice what other studios in Yokohama were paying, with a prospect of earning double the daily rate if he worked on a Sunday, while regular bonuses and gifts were also given.

Nevertheless, Farsari felt obliged to find other ways to motivate his staff. In a letter to his sister, he complained that "the worst part of my profession is the daily raging, swearing, and beating I have to mete out. I do this according to a fixed schedule." Each morning, it seems, Farsari would get up, work himself into a rage, and start berating his staff, starting with the lowly mechanics and operators and then work his way through the rest of the studio, saving the colorists until last. Then, having bullied his Japanese employees to the peak of efficiency, Farsari presumably retired to his office for a well-deserved rest. The fact that such behavior seemed to be expected of a Western employer suggests that attitudes in the Yokohama treaty port had not changed much since Beato's time, when a particularly severe beating administered on

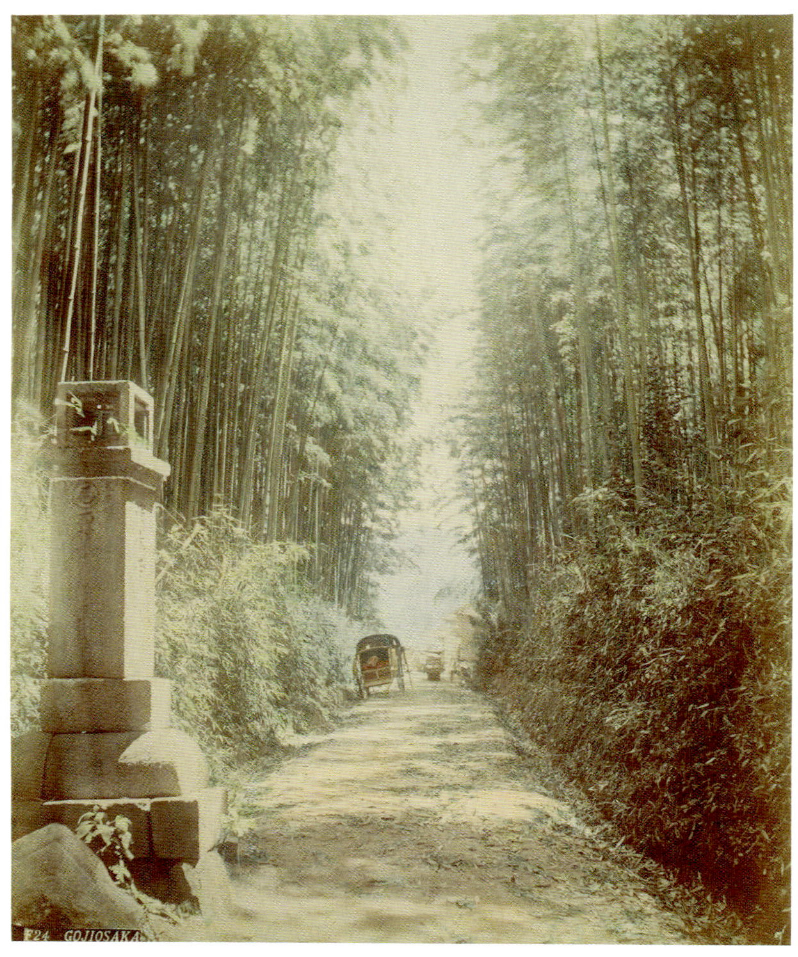

Gojōsaka, Kyoto by Adolfo Farsari

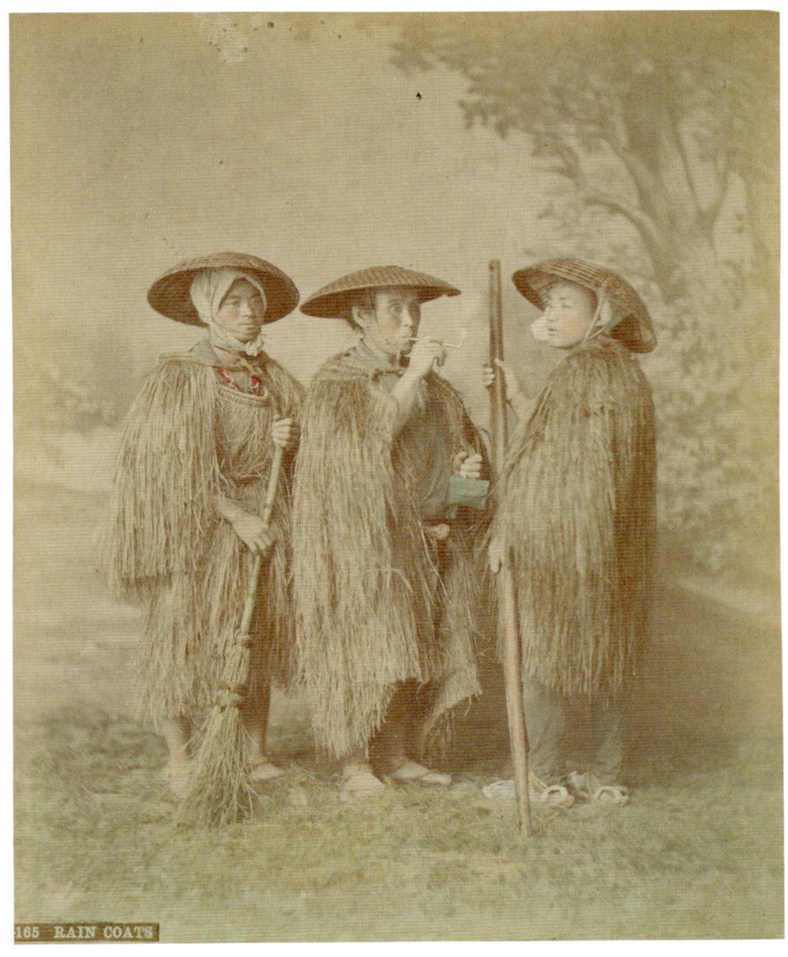

Men in rainwear, by Adolfo Farsari

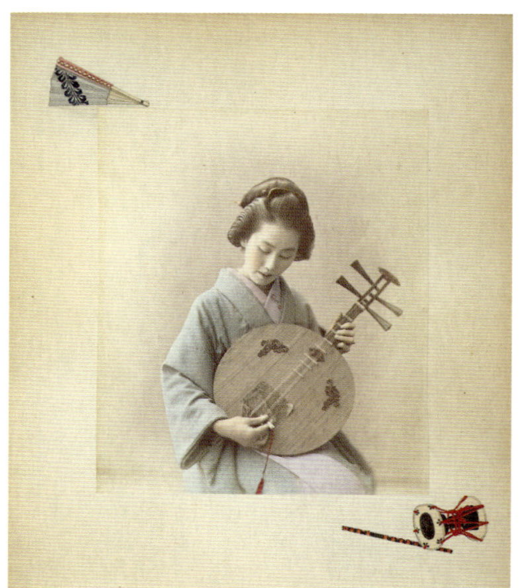

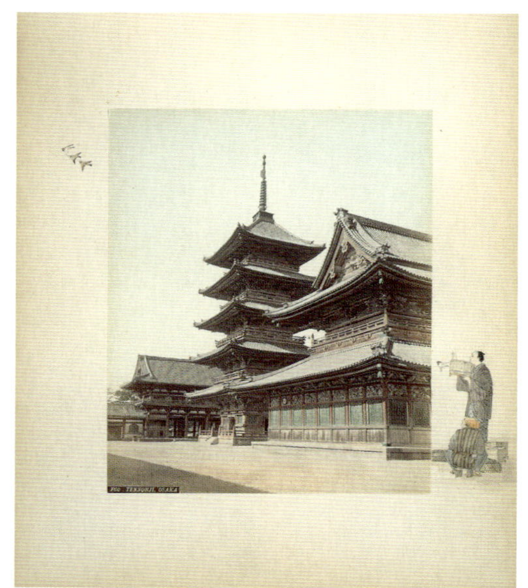

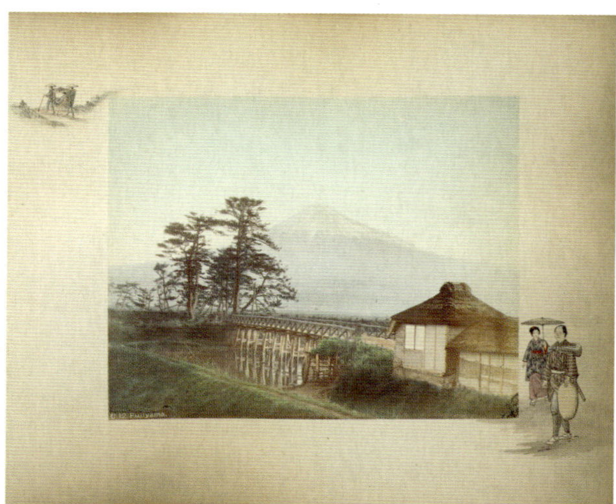

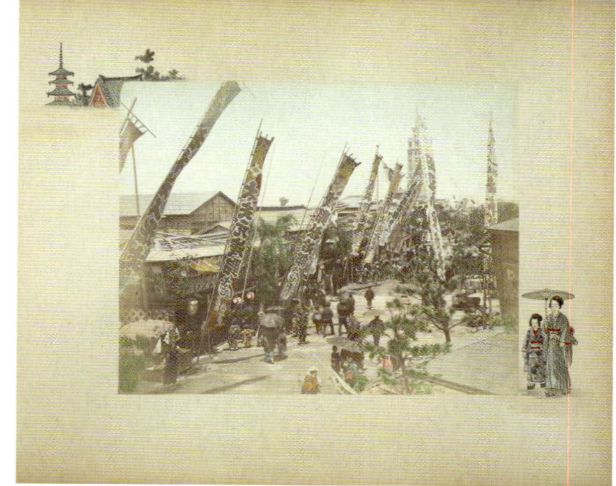

Decorated album pages from the Farsari studio

one of his servants in 1875 had landed the photographer in the British Consular Court. However, in Beato's case, this act was more a result of natural short-temperedness than deliberate policy, and whatever humiliations he inflicted upon his servants, there is no evidence that Beato actually mistreated his Japanese assistants. For Farsari, however, the judicious use of "raging, swearing, and beating" seemed to have the desired effect, and he noted with evident bemusement that his staff referred to him as "the serious one."

To Farsari, it almost seemed destined that Japan should feature in his life. He shared his birthday with the accession date of the first Japanese emperor, Jinmu, and, as a liberal, he applauded the fact that the emperor Meiji should grant the Japanese people their first constitution on this date in 1889: "February 11 was and will be the greatest day this nation ever had and will ever have." Farsari took a Japanese wife with whom he had a daughter, Kiku, in 1885, but preferred to lead a solitary existence. "I live in peace, rather like a misanthrope," he explained to his estranged sister in 1888, "because I associate only with very few people outside of my business relations. I am very well known in this town and enjoy a good reputation. I only want peace, my books and the hope to be able to see you some day." The social life of the foreign community in Yokohama interested Farsari as a spectator rather than a participant, and his outings were confined to visits to the local theater. His perceived ill health was an abiding concern: "I expect to spend most of the winter season on a sofa," he observed, "I don't know why, but in winter I always feel sick without knowing what is wrong with me." Visitors to Farsari's studio often would be received by him wearing a dressing gown, stretched out on a sofa in his office.

Farsari's melancholy contentment was later tinged by homesickness. Signing himself, "Your prodigal son, Adolfo," Farsari sent his first letter home from Yokohama in January 1888, in which he briefly apologized for his long silence and explained what he was doing in Japan. His father's response was guarded, but Farsari's sister, Emma, also wrote in a more sympathetic vein: "Adolfo, there is so much you need to be forgiven for, but you will find our hearts open!" For the next two years, Farsari and his sister exchanged letters almost every week, unwittingly providing future historians of Japanese photography with a unique insight into the workings of the Farsari studio and the psychology of its proprietor. Nostalgia gradually took hold of Farsari, and Italy began to dominate his future plans; recollections of his family, friends, and birthplace appeared with increasing regularity in his letters; he talked of visiting his family in a few years time, perhaps after 1891 when the business could do without him; he made efforts to recover the Italian nationality he had forfeited about 1864 when he had gone to the United States and had joined the Union Army, and, in 1889, presented King Victor Emmanuel II with a deluxe photograph album to improve his chances. Farsari's ambition extended beyond simply regaining an Italian passport — the former New York State Volunteer Cavalry trooper wanted to be a *cavaliere*, or knight of the Italian aristocracy, as well. Farsari believed that such a title would be good for business, but it is possible that he also wanted to stake his claim to the legacy of Baron von Stillfried by securing a noble title of his own.

Suddenly, in April 1890, Farsari left Yokohama for Italy, taking Kiku with him. He was not to see Japan again and died in Vicenza in 1898, four days before his fifty-seventh birthday, in the family home he had often dreamed of visiting. Farsari had arranged for the studio to continue in his absence and may well have planned for it to continue after his death. Surprisingly, when it came time to wind up Farsari's business affairs in Japan, there was little left to send to his family in Italy, though A. Farsari and Company continued to function and, until 1901, Farsari continued to be listed as proprietor. The day-to-day running of the studio had long been entrusted to a Japanese manager, Tonokura Tsunetarō, "an honest man" whom Farsari had known since his partnership with E. A. Sargent in the mid-1870s. Tonokura managed the company until 1901, when he replaced Farsari as outright proprietor. The line of succession was already in place within the company: when Tonokura quit to establish his own studio in 1904, ownership passed to Farsari's former chief operator, Watanabe Tokutarō, who was succeeded in turn in the following year by the former secretary, Fukagawa Itomarō. In 1906, the business was finally registered as a Japanese company and continued to operate until the Great Kanto Earthquake struck Yokohama in 1923.

Farsari's was the last foreign-owned studio of any note in Japan, and his departure from Yokohama in 1890 marked the beginning of the end of the foreign presence in Japanese commercial photography. Symbolically, in 1898, the same year that Farsari died and left his studio to Japanese management, the Yokohama Bund, which had been the address of choice over three decades for Beato, Stillfried, and Farsari, was occupied for the first time by a Japanese photographer, Yamabe Zenjirō, who leased a studio four doors down from A. Farsari and Company's old premises next to the Oriental Hotel. For the remainder of the Meiji era, Japanese photographic studios proliferated in Yokohama: in 1891, the total number of Japanese-owned studios in the city stood at ten; by 1902, it rose to fifteen; and by 1912, twenty such studios were in operation. Among their number were two studios that, established within a year of one another in the early 1880s, came to dominate the Yokohama photographic market in the last two decades of the Meiji era. They were operated by two very different individuals, Kusakabe Kimbei and Tamamura Kōzaburō.

KUSAKABE KIMBEI

Kusakabe Kimbei (1841–1934) was born on October 15, 1841 in Kofu, in present-day Yamanashi Prefecture, as the youngest child and only son in a family of merchants. Unusually for members of the merchant class under the shogunal social system, the Kusakabe family had both the wealth and social connections to qualify for two privileges traditionally regarded as the exclusive preserve of the samurai, namely a surname and the right to carry swords. The family apparently placed few restraints on the young heir apparent, and he was allowed to develop his natural talent for painting. But, when at the age of eighteen, he announced that he intended to go to the newly opened treaty port of Yokohama to become an artist, he encountered, for perhaps the first time in his life, serious parental opposition. The young Kusakabe refused to give up his childhood dream, however, and in 1859 he ran away from home.

What the merchant's son did next in Yokohama is unclear — his name does not appear in any records until almost ten years later, in 1868, when he was listed as an employee of Felice Beato's photographic studio. Significantly, he was recorded then not with the surname of his privileged family, but, like any commoner, simply under his given name. Family oral tradition confirms that Kusakabe joined Beato's studio as an assistant, but gives no date, and the four years between Kusakabe's arrival in Yokohama and that of Beato in 1863 remains a mystery. One possibility is that

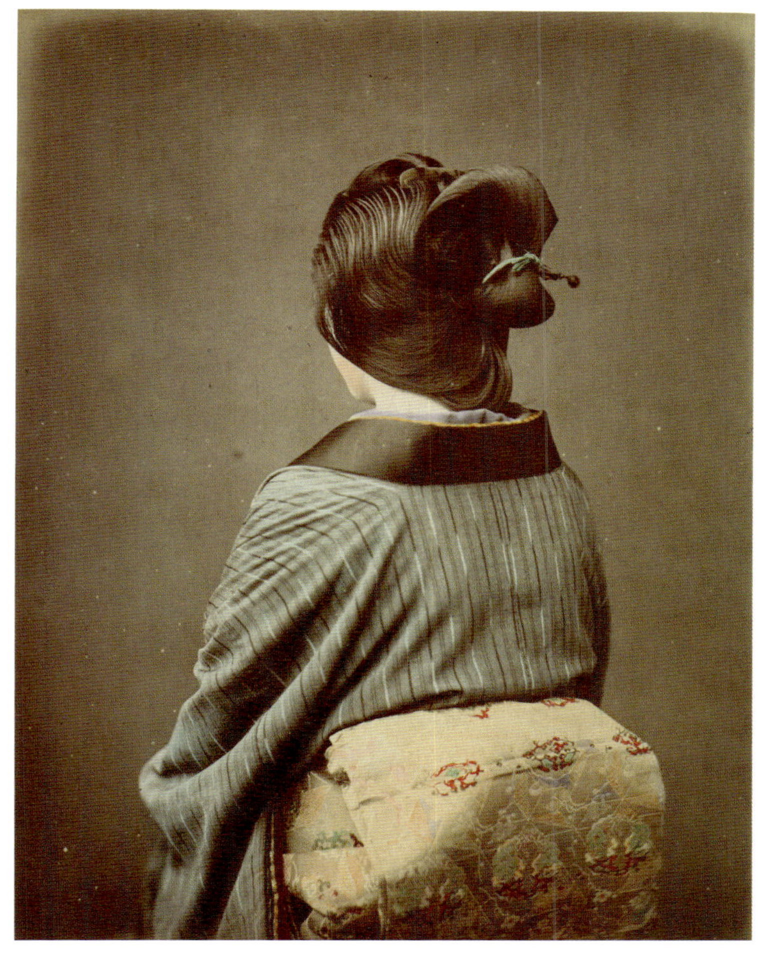

A portrait by Kusakabe Kimbei

Kusakabe chose to go to Yokohama in order to study Western painting. If so, this may have brought him into contact with the artist Charles Wirgman, who as a friend and collaborator of Beato would have been in a position to introduce Kusakabe to him. It is unclear what prompted Kusakabe to abandon the study of painting in favor of photography, but what is certain is that by the late 1860s, Kusakabe was one of Beato's most valued assistants. As such, he may well have simply helped to carry his employer's camera and other photographic equipment on his occasional expeditions to scenic spots; or, especially given his artistic impulses, Kimbei may have been involved in the process of hand-coloring the sepia monochrome prints produced by Beato.

Beato was not the easiest of employers, but he seems to have valued Kusakabe's resourcefulness, and it is evident that a rapport developed between the two men. Family legend would later recall how Kusakabe's quick wits saved Beato from losing one of the more gruesome images in his portfolio.[16] Returning from the local execution ground where Beato and Kusakabe had been photographing the crucified corpse of a recently executed criminal, they were stopped by some officials who had probably watched the pair at work and wanted to inspect the unprocessed negative in Beato's camera. Kusakabe successfully put them off, claiming that, since cameras only recorded images of the virtuous, there was nothing for them to see. We know of another occasion when Beato expressed his appreciation by taking Kusakabe with him on a photographic expedition to Shanghai in the fall of 1867. In an unusual departure, Beato apparently treated his Japanese assistant to a night out on the town, which ended with both of them having to be carried back to their hotel in the British Settlement by the police. Early the following morning, their drunken slumber was interrupted by the bloodcurdling screams of a Chinese woman in the next building undergoing foot binding. Kusakabe's first, and perhaps only, foreign excursion was made even more memorable by the timing of their return journey to Yokohama. Within only two weeks of their arrival home, Shogun Yoshinobu was deposed, thus ending more than two hundred and fifty years of shogunal rule, and power was reclaimed in the name of the emperor. Having left Yokohama in the third year of the Keio era, Beato and Kusakabe returned two months later in December 1867 to find themselves at the eve of the Meiji era.[17]

On his return to Japan, Kusakabe may well have recalled the story of Urashima Taro, the Japanese Rip van Winkel who returned from a visit to another world to find that nothing at home was the same as he had left it. However, the decade or so following the Meiji Restoration presents any would-be biographer of Kusakabe with too many unrecorded or "missing" years to allow any insight into his personal development. At some point in the 1870s, Kusakabe and Beato parted company, and there is a possibility that Kusakabe joined the studio of Beato's former pupil Baron von Stillfried. If so, it cannot have been as pleasant as working for Beato. Stillfried would later reveal a deep-seated suspicion of his Japanese employees and would only instruct them in one particular area of specialization while ensuring that they saw nothing of any other part of the production process. The reason for this, according to an interview Stillfried gave in 1877, was that "at first he used to show his one assistant all the different photographic manipulations necessary to produce a picture, and the consequence was that he soon left and set up on his own account."[18] Was Kusakabe this former employee who had displayed such displeasing initiative? A rare photograph in the possession of Stillfried's descendants pur-

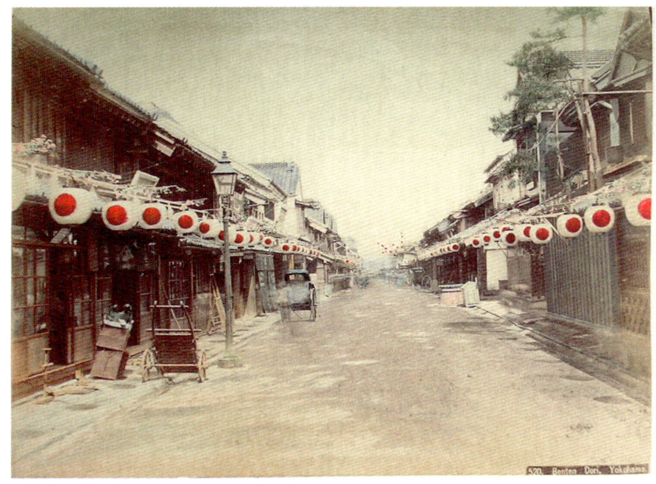

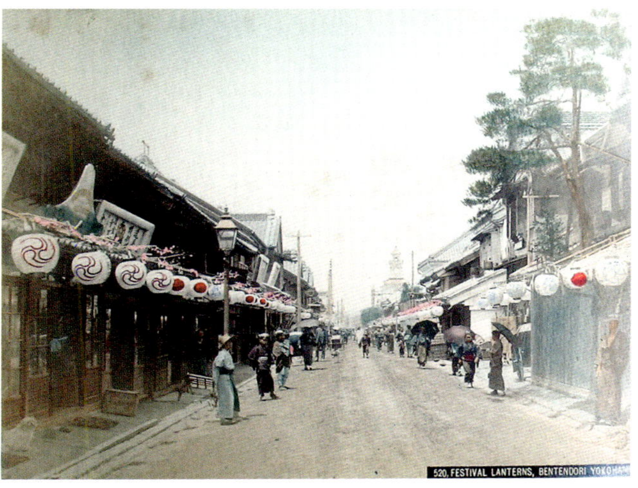

Kusakabe updates his portfolio: Benten-dōri in the mid-1880s (left) and, with the addition of the clock tower, in 1894

ports to show Stillfried and Kusakabe together in a studio setting. Taken at some point in the early 1870s, it shows Stillfried sitting at his easel, apparently in the middle of painting a self-portrait, while amid the surrounding clutter are four cameras. Seated at Stillfried's feet is a Japanese man in traditional dress, still wearing a topknot, whose gaze seems to be directed not so much toward his master as the impressive range of camera equipment behind him. One cannot help suspecting that Kusakabe was indeed the former assistant who left Stillfried's studio before 1877 after learning what he needed to know and whose departure caused Stillfried to ration his knowledge more strictly with his Japanese assistants. If so, this still leaves at least five years of Kusakabe's life unaccounted for, and the first we hear of him as an independent photographer is in 1881.

Through either choice or economic necessity, Kusakabe eschewed the foreign settlement and located his business instead in the so-called Native Town at 26 Benten-dōri, an artery of Yokohama described by one foreign resident as "a bargain-hunter's paradise." Having presumably discovered long ago that his given name presented less difficulty for foreigners to pronounce than his family name, he called his studio "K. Kimbei," and it is evident that from the beginning, Kusakabe sought his clientele from among the numerous foreign tourists who visited Yokohama.

Surprisingly, Kusakabe had little in the way of original work with which to create his first portfolio, and he had to turn to that of another photographer created almost a decade before. Uchida Kuichi's portfolio had been in a state of semi-dormancy since his death in 1875, and Kusakabe somehow succeeded in acquiring a large quantity of Uchida's negatives, probably from his widow. It was an astute move since it gave Kusakabe a solid foundation on which to build his own portfolio of landscapes, and over the next fifteen years, he visited the same locations photographed by Uchida and took his own photographic views. Steadily, Kusakabe's portfolio took on its own flavor, though some images from the Uchida portfolio, as well as a handful he had taken (legally or illegally) from Stillfried and Beato, proved impossible to imitate or drop.

As the portfolio changed, Kusakabe sometimes phased out not only Uchida's negatives, but also some of his own, especially those depicting urban locations such as Yokohama and Tokyo, which were undergoing regular change. One example is a view of Benten-dōri in Yokohama, which Kusakabe originally photographed in the mid-1880s. By 1894, the street was smarter and the skyline somewhat different with the construction of the Kawakita clock tower, and Kusakabe duly took a more up-to-date view of the street. It was also an opportunity to show how he had developed as a photographer, and Kusakabe seems to have chosen to replicate features from the old photograph, such as the festival lanterns hanging outside the buildings, in order to emphasize the difference, for whereas the original view is devoid of any sense of bustle, Kusakabe carefully staged the new scene to give the impression of townspeople going about their daily business.

His success enabled the studio to extend its reach. In 1887, he established a branch studio at 20 Hinodechō in Yokohama, and soon afterward opened a Tokyo branch at 9 Shinsenza. Around the year 1890, he moved his main studio to the so-called Main Street of Yokohama at Honchō-dōri, an even more popular destination than Benten-dōri for visitors in search of curios and souvenirs.[19] At the height of the studio's success, Kusakabe was employing more than thirty members of staff, to whom he offered evening classes in *kanji* (the Japanese writing system based on characters borrowed from Chinese), calligraphy, and English every other day.

In 1914, at the age of seventy-three, Kusakabe finally retired from photography and entrusted his business affairs to his son-in-law, the photographer Ogawa Sashichi. He spent a peaceful retirement pursuing his boyhood love of painting, interrupted only by the chaos of the Great Kanto Earthquake of 1923, which Kusakabe and his family survived. Around 1930, poor health forced him to move to Ashiya, near Kobe, where he lived with his favorite granddaughter, Tama, and her family. For a man who had spent his career combining Western technology with traditional Japanese culture, it was perhaps appropriate that Tama should have married Frank Luther, a German-Japanese, and Kusakabe's final years were spent in the Luther household surrounded by his great-grandchildren. He died in 1934 and received a Christian burial in Ashiya.

THE COMMERCIAL PHOTOGRAPHER: TAMAMURA KŌZABURŌ

Tamamura Kōzaburō (1856–?) remains a shadowy figure in Japanese photographic history. The few portraits of him that survive show a rather austere individual, his aloofness enhanced by an unflattering pair of pince-nez eyeglasses. He has attracted surprisingly little attention from present-day photo-historians, even failing to appear at all in some recent surveys of Japanese photography. During his lifetime, however, Tamamura was one of the most successful commercial photographers in Japan, and an important rival to Kusakabe Kimbei.

Tamamura was born in Edo in 1856 into a family which had a long tradition of serving as hereditary retainers to the head priest of the main temple at Nikkō, Rinnōji, and it is likely that the young Tamamura would also have entered the temple's service had not the head priest's position been abolished in 1868 with the Meiji Restoration. By then, however, Tamamura had developed an interest in photography, and around the time of the overthrow of the shogunal government, he began his apprenticeship with a local photographer. Tamamura's education was different from that of his contemporary, Kusakabe Kimbei, who at this time was learning photography in Yokohama while working for Felice Beato. Tamamura's formative years as a student and then as a photographer in his own right were spent instead in his hometown, since renamed Tokyo. Tamamura's teacher was not a foreigner but Kanamaru Genzo, who operated a studio near a ford on the Sumida River in the Asakusa district. In 1874, after almost seven years of training, the precocious Tamamura, still in his teens, opened his own studio in the nearby Okuyama area. It was not until 1882 that Tamamura moved to Yokohama, occupying premises on Benten-dōri from which he would operate his business for more than thirty years. In that same year, his studio received an important commission from an unidentified tea exporter to take a series of photographs illustrating the production and processing of tea, as well as a parallel commission to photograph the cultivation of silk worms and silk manufacture.

Tamamura's greatest success, however, was in catering to the same foreign market as Kusakabe Kimbei. It was probably with an eye to this market and its gravitation toward foreign-owned studios that he entered into a partnership with Farsari in 1885 to buy out the Japan Photographic Association on the Bund. How long this partnership lasted is unclear, but it is evident that within a few years, Tamamura was presenting serious competition to the Farsari studio, boasting an inventory of about 1,200 negatives.

As Tamamura's profile rose, so did the studio's. In 1890, he renamed it the Gyokushindō, contracting the main kanji characters from his family name and the word *shashin* into a classical sounding reading, and adding the kanji character *dō*, indicating a hall. This was probably intended to impart some tone to the enterprise, but it was a curious step to take in a market where most photographers operated under their own family names, or even, in Kusakabe's case, their given name. Although in use for about eight years, the name never really caught on, especially among foreign clients, and in 1898, Tamamura reverted to using "K. Tamamura, Art Photographer."

On July 19, 1896 one of the daily newspapers published a report that the Tamamura studio had received an order from a merchant in Boston called "Shiretto" (a misreading of the Boston publisher J. B. Millet) for one million photographs of the scenery and people of Japan. In order to complete the first batch of forty thousand prints in various formats, Tamamura had employed an extra 105 members of staff, and he expected to have the next installment of 180,000 prints ready for shipment within the month. The figure of one million was almost certainly an exaggeration, possibly made up by Tamamura himself for publicity purposes, but it was a huge order nonetheless. The photographs ordered by Millet were intended for an ambitious multivolume publication edited by Francis Brinkley and entitled, *Japan: Described and Illustrated*, one of the last great books to be illustrated with original albumen print photographs. During the years 1897 and 1898, the work was published in various limited editions, and for fourteen of the sixteen editions produced we know that 151,500 large-format photographs and 254,000 small-format photographs were hand-colored and later tipped into 37,750 individual volumes.[20] It was no coincidence that exports of photographs from Yokohama in 1896 rose to the highest level ever recorded, representing a staggering five-fold increase from the previous year. Even this figure does not do true justice to the impact of Millet's order — in 1895, exports of photographs from Japanese studios to the United States had totaled 639 yen; by the end of 1896, the total was a mind-boggling 20,434 yen, which, even when taking into account the share occupied by Tamamura's rivals, represented an enormous turnover for his studio.

One suspects that, as far as Tamamura was concerned, photography interested him less as an artistic endeavor than as a potentially lucrative business, and it would fall to his son Kihei to explore new currents in Japanese artistic photography. For Tamamura Senior, it seems, the balance sheet was more important. In 1898, his tax burden was the highest of any studio in Yokohama, and, on a national level, second only to that of the Tokyo-based distributor Konishi.[21] Indeed, Tamamura was more of a photographic supplier than a photographer, for of the 164 yen he paid in tax for that year, only 29 yen was payable on actual photographic work, with the remainder derived from the sale of photographic supplies. When compared with other photographic studios, this figure shows that sales of Tamamura's photographs, while the highest for any studio in Yokohama, were lower than his rivals in Tokyo, such as Ogawa Kazuma (84 yen, 70 sen) and Nakajima Matsuchi (38 yen, 15 sen). In 1909, Tamamura received more gratifying publicity when his was reported to be the highest tax-paying photographic business in Japan, and, in the following year, Tamamura was elected chairman of the Yokohama Confederation of Professional Photographers (Yokohama Shashingyō Kumiai). Yokohama remained the focus of his business. In 1903, Tamamura opened a branch establishment in Kobe, which seems to have operated successfully until around 1910, when Tamamura allowed the manager, who was a former pupil, to buy him out.

The considerable commercial success Tamamura enjoyed in the final decades of the Meiji era was achieved at a price. Behind the hyperbole of an advertisement in English, his basic strategy of undercutting the competition was plain: Tamamura offered "the finest photographs in native costume, the finest collection of views, the finest colored views, the largest collection, the largest studio, the best artists," and promised "better than all, THE LOWEST PRICES." This could only be achieved at the expense of quality. One client, the British naturalist Richard Gordon Smith, left some of his own work at Tamamura's studio in Yokohama for coloring in 1901, and recorded his dismay at the result in his diary: "Went to Tamamura (photographer) this morning for my colored photographs of Burma. They were badly done. The moment a Japanese leaves his country he can neither paint nor think."[22] After a second visit to Tamamura, Smith found himself not only disappointed but also looking back wistfully to the days of extra-territoriality: "Developed photographs with Tamamura; the ass let in too much light and spoiled most of them. I would have given a good deal for the privilege of knocking him down, but here in Japan that means from between three and six months' imprisonment, without the option of a fine."[23]

It was almost certainly his former business partner Tamamura that Farsari had in mind when he wrote despairingly, "there are in Japan two or three photographers who paint prints, but they are horrible . . . Just imagine, a Japanese paints sixty photographs — very badly — a day!" Farsari was not exaggerating the contrast with his own studio, where each artist's output averaged two or three photographs a day. The 1896 report of Tamamura's special order from Millet gives a valuable snapshot of how intensively he expected his colorists to work. Even assuming that all 105 temporary employees were colorists, and that they worked seven days a week, this would require each worker to color an average of fifty-seven photographs a day in order to complete the order within the thirty days promised. Since obviously not all the workers would be employed as colorists, but would also be engaged in printing and copying, the required daily output of a colorist would easily exceed the total of sixty per day, which caused Farsari such consternation, and, which, as he pointed out, could only occur at the expense of quality. Doubtless Tamamura was aware of the five hundred dollar challenge that Farsari presented to his competitors to match the quality of his work, and he was presumably content to let Farsari keep his money while he made the most of this unprecedented bulk order.

Tamamura's subsequent life and career remain a mystery. In 1916, his son Kihei took over the studio and continued to run it until around the time of the Great Kanto Earthquake of 1923. It is not clear whether the Tamamura studio was among those destroyed in the catastrophe, or indeed whether Tamamura Senior was still alive at this time, but the family fortune was almost certainly lost. Although the business continued to appear in the local trade directory until 1925, it was around this time that Tamamura Kihei left Yokohama and moved to Osaka, where he was employed by the Mitsukoshi Department Store to manage their photographic department. By this time, Tamamura Senior was probably dead and, therefore, spared seeing his son reduced to working in the U.S. Army's PX Stores after Japan's surrender in 1945. In 1951, Tamamura Kihei himself passed away.

THE DECLINE OF YOKOHAMA PHOTOGRAPHY

For almost two decades, photography in Yokohama was a thriving business, but from the first years of the twentieth century, it quickly entered a period of decline. Exports of photographs from Japan generally began to fall after 1899, and in 1901, for the first time, Yokohama ceded its hitherto dominant share of the export market to Kobe. However, far from indicating that Kobe was developing as a rival photographic center, this fall in exports from Yokohama merely indicated that the production of photographs specifically for export was in general decline; as the center of this trade, Yokohama was simply the first city to suffer the effects of the downturn.[24]

Several factors ensured that this downward trend was irreversible. For some time, the smart money had been on photomechanical processes. In 1888, the photographer Ogawa Kazumasa had established the first collotype print works in Tokyo and, by 1890, was printing his collotypes in color. Tamamura also augmented his stock with collotype albums. Not only were collotype photographs cheaper to produce than albumen photographs, but images created photomechanically also possessed greater consistency, especially with regard to color permanence, and the popular selling point of "colors which never fade" contrasted with the irregular quality of coloring found with hand-tinted albumen prints.

If the threat presented by collotype albums was not a sufficient cause of concern for the more traditional photographic studio, more difficult to ignore was the increasing popularity of picture postcards. On October 1, 1900, the Ministry of Communications authorized the use of privately manufactured postcards for postal purposes, thus allowing picture postcards to be used for the first time. From around this period, Yokohama was deluged with hand-colored picture postcards, which, retailing at between two and ten *sen* each, were affordable souvenirs that could be kept in an album in the same way as the Yokohama *shashin*, but in far greater quantities, or else posted to friends and family. Photographic views and portraits began to be printed more frequently as postcards than as albumen prints, and even the Kusakabe studio and A. Farsari and Company began to produce photographic views as collotype-printed postcards alongside their established output. By the end of the Meiji era, Yokohama was the center of Japan's burgeoning postcard industry.

Another challenge to commercial photographers in Yokohama and elsewhere in Japan was the rise of amateur photography. Amateur photographers — both Japanese and foreign — were nothing new in Japan, but they had generally been limited to narrow social groups, such as the Japanese nobility, the officer class of the Western powers' armed forces, and the cadre of foreigners working for the Japanese government. From the 1880s, however, it was becoming increasingly common for globetrotters in Japan to take their own pictures with their own equipment. One wealthy tourist and amateur photographer, the Frenchman Hugues Krafft, even earned a place in Japanese photographic history in 1882 by being the first to take pictures in Japan using the newly developed dry plate process. His portfolio of around three hundred negatives provided a uniquely personal record of the people and scenery he encountered during a five-month tour of Japan, which encompassed Nagasaki, Kobe, Yokohama, Tokyo, Nikkō, the Tōkaidō, and the Nakasendō.[25] His experience showed that with the more flexible dry plate process, whereby presensitized glass negatives were ready for immediate use, amateur photographers could take pictures while on the move. By comparison, the wet plate process, which required the sensitizing, exposing, and fixing of a glass-plate negative to be completed within minutes of one another, was more cumbersome and less spontaneous. Finally, in 1899, the manufacture of celluloid roll film by George Eastman to accompany his Kodak camera — "You press the button, we do the rest" — brought photography within the reach of everybody, and the amateur photographer, no longer burdened with glass negatives and chemicals, could venture even farther afield.

Farsari was quick to notice the amateur photography trend: by his own estimate, in 1889, around half of all visitors to Yokohama were amateur photographers, and he found that the only way to get them into his studio was to set aside a darkroom for them to use free of charge. Whether they bought anything, of course, was a different matter. For the remainder of the Meiji era, photographic studios had to adapt to the needs of amateur photographers as best they could. In 1898, the tax on sales of photographic supplies at Tamamura's studio accounted for more than eighty percent of the total amount of tax he paid that year, and by the following decade, like Kusakabe, he was offering his clients a developing, printing, and hand-coloring service. By 1905, Kusakabe was advertising himself as an "Importer of Cameras, Kodaks, Films and Supplies, also Exporter of Japanese Colored Photographs, Lantern Slides and Curios."

Also contributing to the decline of the Yokohama photographic trade was the removal of travel restrictions in Japan in 1899 following the reversal of the so-called Unequal Treaties that had originally opened Japan to foreign trade in 1858. Each of the areas set aside for foreign settlement had been enclosed by "treaty limits" within a radius of ten *ri* (approximately forty kilometers) from the center, and foreigners wishing to travel outside these areas to more remote parts of Japan had had to apply to the Japanese Ministry of Foreign Affairs for a special passport, citing either ill health or research as the justification for their journey. The removal of these restrictions in 1899 opened up the interior of Japan and did much to demystify the subject matter of the Yokohama *shashin*. The "unbeaten tracks"[26] pursued by an intrepid visitor such as Isabella Bird in 1878, were, by 1900, within relatively easy reach, and whereas commercial photographers had previously played a major role in introducing and interpreting the sights of Japan's exotic interior to foreign tourists, their intermediary role became redundant when tourists could see these sights for themselves and take their own photographs.

The careers of Farsari, Kusakabe, and Tamamura offer valuable insights into the genre of the Yokohama *shashin* in both its heyday and the period of its decline. Each photographer may have approached his practice in a different way, but taken together as three particularly successful practitioners of commercial photography in Yokohama in the Meiji era, their combined experience reveals much about the interaction between the artistic and commercial aspects of the genre. Having long been dismissed as kitsch, the artistic value and historical significance of their work is currently undergoing re-evaluation, and it is hoped that this book and the exhibition it accompanies will contribute to the recognition of Yokohama *shashin* as an important current in Japanese art.

1. *Humphrey's Journal of Photography and the Allied Arts and Sciences*, v. 19, no. 18 (January 15, 1868): 287.

2. This figure is based on an analysis of the table of Yokohama-based photographers compiled by Saitō Takio; see his "Yokohama no shashinka ichiran," in Saitō Takio, ed., *Saishoku arubamu—Meiji no Nihon—"Yokohama shashin" no sekai* (Yokohama: Yurindo, 1990), 236–41, with cross-references made to Torin Boyd and Izakura Naomi, *Portraits in Sepia from the Japanese Carte de Visite Collection of Torin Boyd and Naomi Izakura / Sepia—iro no shōzō—Bakumatsu-Meiji meishiban shashin korekushon* (Tokyo: Asahi Sonorama, 2000).

3. Beato's birth years are now beyond doubt, based on an application for a passport he made in 1858, when he was going to India. The application is in Record Book, "India, Political Consultations March 19–April 9, 1858," P/202/49, no. 244, India Office Archives, British Library, London. An unusually early example of Beato's work in the collection of the Japan Society of London indicates that by the end of 1863, he was offering his clients photographs in Japanese stitched albums. The album, acquired by Lieutenant Alexander D. Douglas of the Royal Navy, bears the date "December 20 1863" on the front endpaper, and contains forty-eight photographs from Beato's studio and three watercolors, which, although unsigned, are most likely the work of Charles Wirgman. The earliest known portfolio of Japanese photographs, consisting of at least eighty-five numbered views, was put on sale in Yokohama in the fall of 1862 by the Shanghai-based photographer William Saunders. These photographs, however, appear to have been sold individually rather than in an album format; see "Mr. Saunders' photographic views in Japan," *Japan Herald*, October 25, 1862.

4. The best example of this format is the pair of albums in the Victoria and Albert Museum.

5. William Griffis, *The Mikado's Empire* (New York: Harper & Brothers, 1876), 344.

6. Luke Gartlan, "Changing Views: The Early Topographical Photographs of Stillfried and Company," *Koshashin kenkyū* (Sainsbury Institute for the Study of Japanese Arts and Cultures/Nagasaki University Library), v. 2 (March 2003): 16–29. Also in *Reflecting Truth: Japanese Photography in the Nineteenth Century*, ed. Nicole Coolidge Rousmaniere and Mikiko Hirayama (Norwich, England: Sainsbury Institute for the Study of Japanese Arts and Cultures, forthcoming 2004).

7. It is on record that these albums were acquired by the Navy Ministry as a special purchase; see Kasumikaikan Shiryōtenji-iinkai, ed., *Rokumeikan hizō shashinchō* (Tokyo: Heibonsha, 1997), 196–240.

8. Quoted in Luke Gartlan, "A Chronology of Baron Raimund von Stillfried-Ratenicz (1839–1911)," in John Clark, ed., *Japanese Exchanges in Art, 1850s–1930s, with Britain, Continental Europe, and the U.S.A.* (Sydney: Power Publications, 2001), 137–38.

9. Advertisement in W. E. L. Keeling, *Tourist's Guide to Yokohama, Tokio, Hakone, Fujiyama, Kamakura, Yokoska, Kanozan, Narita, Nikko, Kioto, Osaka, Etc., Etc.* (Tokyo: A. Farsari, 1880).

10. This and further quotes from Farsari are based on the translations given in Lia Beretta, "Adolfo Farsari: An Italian Photographer in Meiji Japan," *Transactions of the Asiatic Society of Japan*, v. 11 (1996): 33–48. Beretta's monograph is based on a collection of family letters discovered in Italy by Elena Dal Pra.

11. "Gaijin haiso," *Jiji Shimbun*, September 6, 1886, cited in Saitō Takio, *Saishoku alubamu*, 230. Strangely, no further connection between Farsari and Tamamura emerges from contemporary sources, and one can only speculate what happened after Farsari bought out the Yokohama Photographic Company.

12. *Photographic Times and American Photographer*, July 22, 1887. Quoted in Gartlan, "A Chronology of Baron Raimund von Stillfried-Ratenicz," 174.

13. Hugh Cortazzi and George Webb, eds., *Kipling's Japan: Collected Writings* (London: Athlone Press, 1988), 92.

14. Ibid., 93.

15. W. K. Burton, "Photography in Japan," *British Journal of Photography*, v. 34 (August 19, 1887): 1424, 519.

16. This and other episodes from family legend were recorded by the researcher Matsumoto Itsuya during interviews with Kusakabe's 103-year-old granddaughter, Uchida Tama, in 1992; see Matsumoto Itsuya, *Bakumatsu Hyōryū* (Tokyo: Nigen to Rekishi sha, 1993).

17. Kusakabe, or his descendants, later retold the story of his journey to Shanghai to make it coincide exactly with the official adoption of the name of the new reign in September 1868.

18. Quoted in the *British Journal of Photography*, v. 24 (November 1877): 914, 536.

19. The popularity of the less salubrious attractions along Honchō-dōri, and especially the "Number Nine" brothel to which it led, may have been the source of the slang expression "hunky dory," indicative of good times, and was apparently coined by foreign sailors on shore leave.

20. Denise Bethel, "The J. B. Millet Company's *Japan: Described and Illustrated by the Japanese*," *Image*, v. 34, nos. 1–2 (1991): 3–22.

21. Nihon Shashin Kyōkai, ed., *Nihon shashinshi nenpyō 1778–1975/9* (Tokyo: Kōdansha, 1976), 114.

22. Richard Gordon Smith's diary entry for March 15, 1901, in Victoria Manthorpe, ed., *The Japan Diaries of Richard Gordon Smith* (London: Rainbird Publishing, 1986), 48.

23. Smith's diary entry for May 1, 1901, ibid., 67.

24. Saitō Takio, "Yokohama shashin no sekai," in Saitō, *Saishoku alubamu*, 244.

25. Hugues Krafft's account of his journey was originally published in 1885 and contained only twenty-four reproductions of the photographs he took during his travels; see Hugues Krafft, *Souvenirs de notre tour du monde* (Paris: Hachette, 1885). The extensive portfolio of photographs that Krafft took in Japan remained virtually unknown until 1996, when it was rediscovered in the Musée Le Vergeur in his hometown of Rheims among a large bequest he had made to a local antiquarian society. To date, Krafft's work has only been published in Japanese; see Gotō Kazuo, ed., *Hugues Krafft: Bonjūru Japon, Furansu seinen ga kassha shita 1882-nen* (Tokyo: Asahi Shimbunsha, 1998).

25. Isabella Bird, *Unbeaten Tracks in Japan* (London: John Murray, 1880).

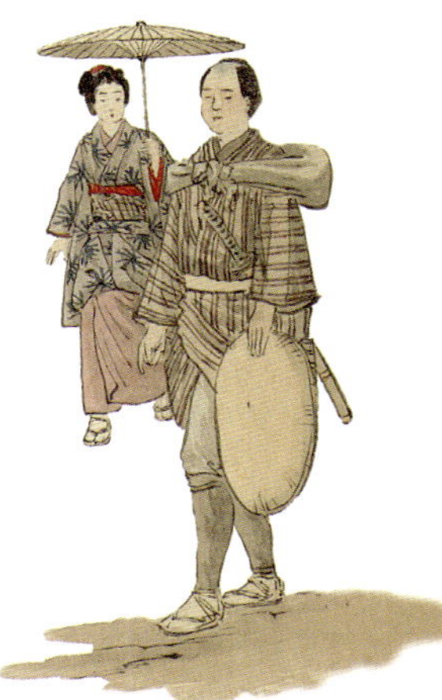

Souvenirs of "Old Japan"

Meiji-era Photography and the Meisho Tradition

ANNE NISHIMURA MORSE

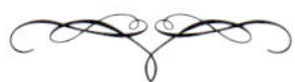

DURING THE SECOND HALF OF THE NINETEENTH CENTURY, many Westerners disillusioned by the rapid industrialization of their own countries conceived of Japan as a simpler place unsullied by the problems of contemporary life. One even described it as "the nearest earthly approach to Paradise or to Lotus-land."[1] Ironically, Japan at that time was striving to transform itself through an ambitious campaign of modernization into a "New Japan" that would be taken seriously by other nations, while simultaneously capitalizing on the West's romanticized notion of an "Old Japan."[2]

Photographs created for the Western market became important souvenirs of the foreigners' encounters with the Japanese archipelago. Among them, views of famous scenic places formed a distinct category, providing the tourist's experience with an aura of unmediated authenticity compared to the staged and stereotyped scenes of Japanese people wearing traditional costumes, or of so-called curiosities, such as jinikishas. An examination of the indigenous Japanese pictorial tradition of famous places, called *meisho*, makes it clear, however, that the selection of the individual sites and the iconography of these nineteenth-century photographs of Japan were informed by a variety of sources. Many photographs showed places that had been celebrated in Japanese art and literature for centuries; others were of locations whose reputations were more recently established.

THE FORGOTTEN TRADITIONS OF CLASSICAL MEISHO

As early as the second half of the ninth century, the Japanese recognized images of famous scenic places (*meisho-e*) as a defined genre.[3] In the highly literary society of the Heian-period (794–1185) imperial court, artists' depiction of *meisho* were inextricably linked with how those places were celebrated in poetic anthologies, such as the Kokinshū, or in narratives, such as the *Tales of Ise* and the *Tale of Genji*. For the viewer's part, the appreciation of the images depended largely on his or her ability to recognize the visual markers within a given composition that carried specific literary allusions.

A recently published Meiji-period photograph, taken in Kobe probably in the 1890s, permits us to examine the relationship between photographs of scenic places in Meiji Japan and this classical *meisho* tradition. In the image, three jinrikishas transporting elegant kimono-clad women pause along a newly constructed

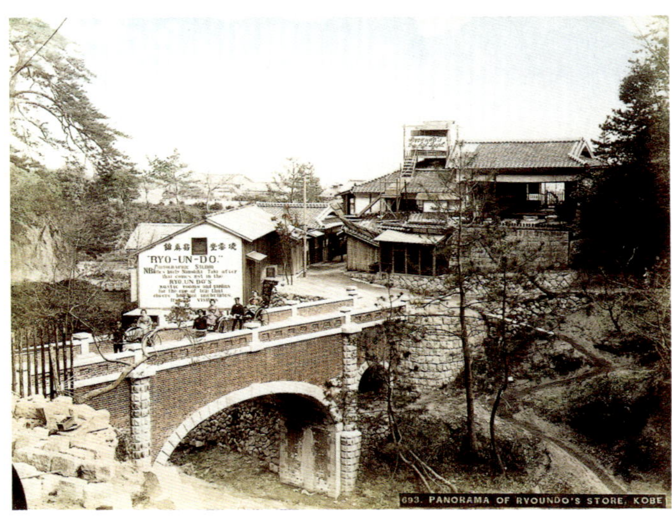

Ryōundō Photo Studio, Ryōundō Photo Studio near Nunobiki Falls *(1890s)*

Western-style brick bridge, and a small cluster of more traditional low-lying wooden structures is visible in the background. The center of the photograph is dominated by an enormous sign written directly on the plaster wall of one of these buildings and that looms over the figures on the bridge. Across the top are the characters *Ryōundō shashinkan*. A lengthy text in English explains: "'Ryo-un-do.' Photographic Studio. NB Kobe's lovely Nunobiki Taki. After come rest in the Ryo-un-do's rustic rooms and gardens for the cup of tea that cheers but not inebriates. Free to visitors."[4]

Any foreign tourist venturing into the Ryoundō doubtless would have been encouraged to purchase photographic images of Nunobiki Taki, or Nunobiki Falls, the spectacular waterfall that had been admired since at least the tenth century when it figured in a well-known section of the *Tales of Ise*. According to this Heian-period text, an excursion to the site had provided an excuse for a poetry-writing contest. One of the guests, a commander of the guards, had recited:

> Which, I wonder, is higher —
> This waterfall or the fall of my tears
> As I wait in vain,
> Hoping today or tomorrow
> To rise in the world.

The host, a minor official, contributed his own poem:

> It looks as though someone
> Must be unstringing
> Those clear cascading gems.
> Alas! My sleeves are too narrow
> To hold them all.[5]

The appreciation of the site by educated Japanese of the Meiji era would have been colored by their knowledge of the poems. Although they may not have been able to recite them, they would have recognized the association of the place with classical literature. (An analogy might be an English or American tourist's visit to the castle at Elsinor, which inevitably evokes thoughts of Shakespeare's *Hamlet*.) To foreign tourists who had little understanding of Japanese poetry, however, the waterfall could have been apprehended only as a natural wonder. In fact, a contemporary travel account merely describes the site in the following

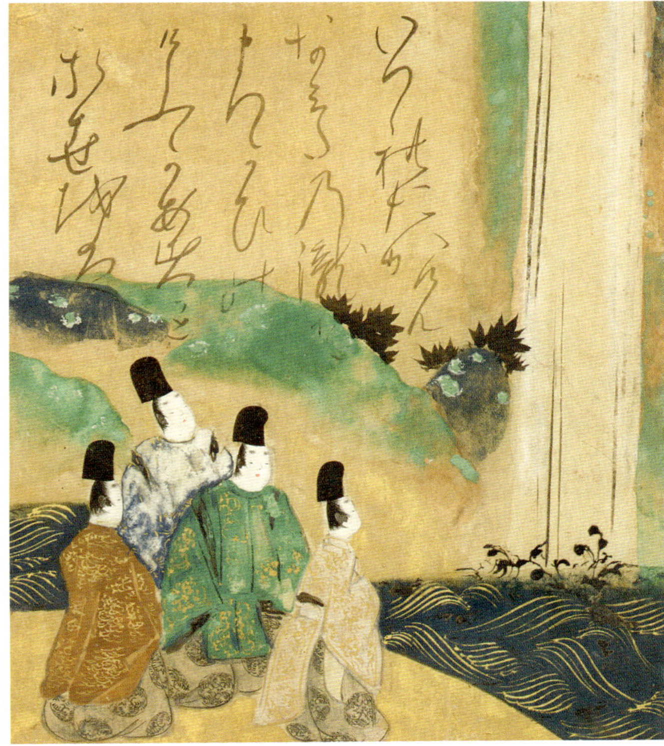

Tawaraya Sōtatsu, Nobles viewing the Nunobiki Waterfall *(about 1642)*

terms: "a clear mountain stream takes two long plunges down sheer granite walls, drops in foaming cascades past old rice-mills, and courses on over the sloping plain to the sea."[6] English-language guidebooks also provide only practical suggestions: "Ladies are advised only to visit Nunobiki under the escort of gentlemen, as the tea-houses are apt to be noisy."[7] The foreign tourist was never informed of the cultural importance of the place.

Kusakabe Kimbei and Adolfo Farsari did take images of Nunobiki — images that did not center on the waterfall but on the teahouses. In reviewing the subjects of most scenic site photography, despite the strong poetic allusions of the places, not surprisingly we find that classical and historic themes were very rarely evoked. Images of Suma or Akashi, known from the *Tale of Genji*, abound in paintings for domestic consumption, but there are few equivalents among Meiji photographs.

SCENES IN AND AROUND THE ANCIENT CAPITAL

Meiji-era photographs may have been little affected by the early poetic or literary traditions of the imperial court, but the photographers' decision to shoot particular *meisho* must have derived from the status that these places had as being visually or historically significant — a status established long before the arrival of the foreign tourist. A preference for photographs of certain sites in the ancient capital of Kyoto, for example, was certainly influenced by traditional *meisho* images depicted in a genre of screen painting known as "Scenes in and Around the Capital" (*rakuchū rakugai*). Produced during the sixteenth and early seventeenth centuries, a long period of civil unrest in which generations of warlords vied for military and political control of the city, such screens present a bird's-eye view of Kyoto and its immediate environs. The eastern and southern sections of the metropolis are depicted on the right hand of the pair of screens; the northern and western on the left. While the screens are panoramic in their scope, emphasis is put on specific places within the city. Popular religious establishments,

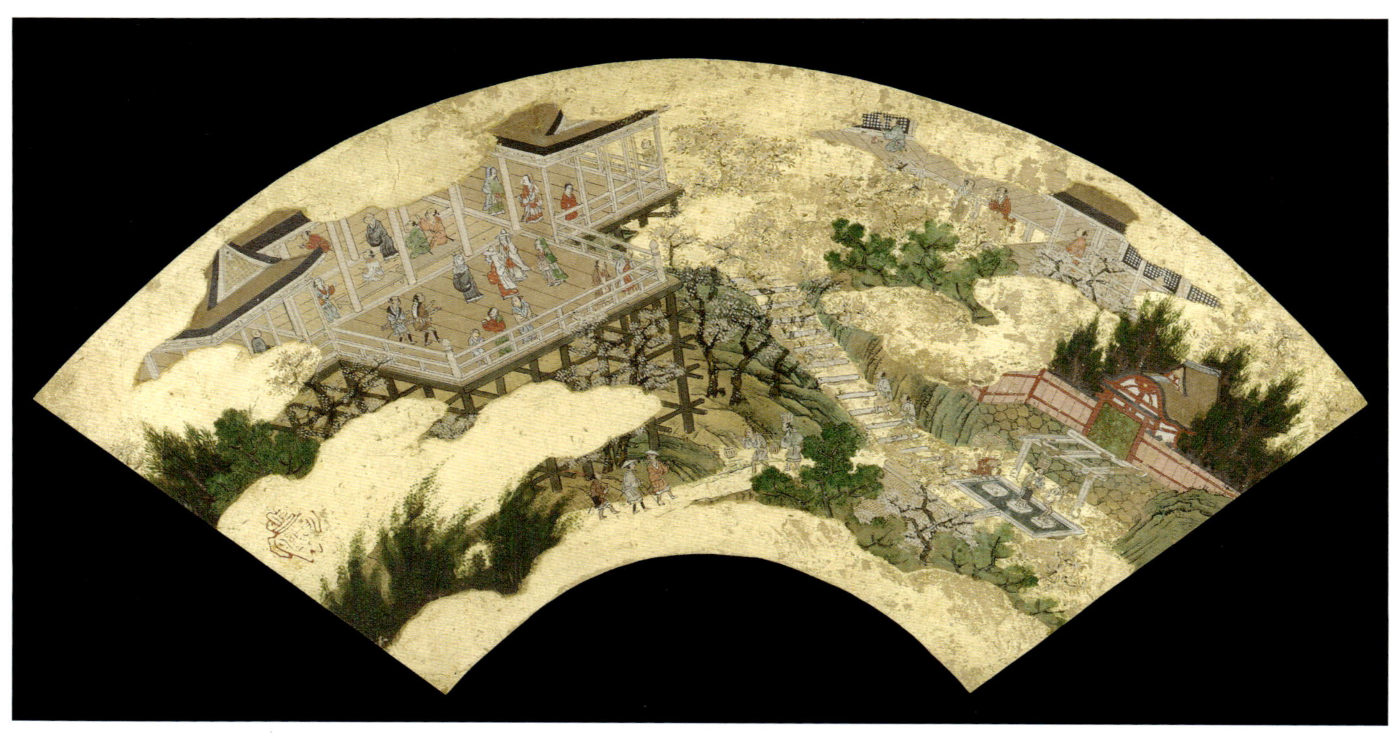

Above: A sixteenth-century fan painting by Kano Shōei depicting Kiyomizudera. Opposite page: The same site by an unknown Meiji-era photographer.

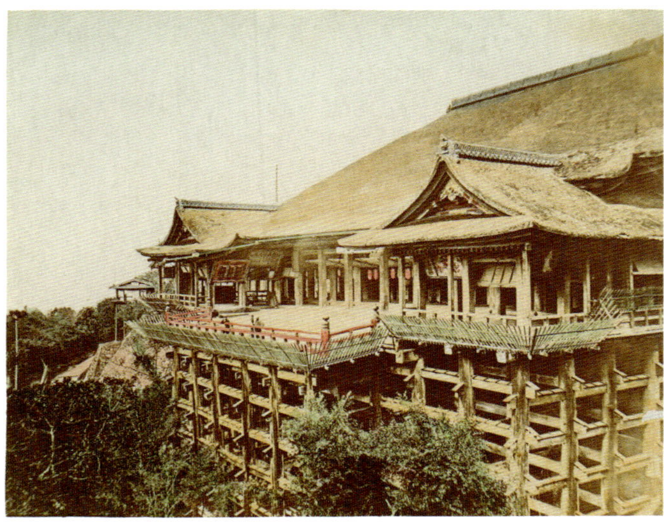

such as Kiyomizudera and the Sanjūsangendō, are always given prominence; the inclusion of other sacred and secular sites generally reflects the politics of the person who commissioned or received specific screens.[8]

Meiji-era artists photographed many of these same "scenes in and around the ancient capital," employing the iconography established by the early paintings. For example, Kiyomizudera, a popular center for the worship of Eleven-headed Kannon, emphasized the wooden scaffolding on which the main hall rested, just as the screens did. Kinkakuji (known as the "Golden Pavilion"), the grand three-storied retreat of the fifteenth-century ruler Ashikaga Yoshimitsu, and the Moon-Crossing Bridge that traversed the cherry and maple trees lining the Katsura River were always photographed from the same vantage point that had been adopted in paintings of Kyoto *meisho*. Thus, while photographers could have imposed a more modern image of the city, the locations they portrayed and the manner in which they depicted them rooted their pictures in tradition.

MOUNT FUJI AND EDO MEISHO

For most tourists arriving by ship, Mount Fuji provided their first glimpse of Japan. Isabella Bird, the celebrated British explorer, described the beauty of the peak in her travel account, *Unbeaten Tracks in Japan: An Account of Travels in the Interior, Including Visits to the Aborigines of Yezo and the Shrine of Nikko*: "[I]t was a wonderful vision, and shortly, as a vision, vanished . . . I never saw a mountain rise in such lonely majesty, with nothing near or far to detract from its height and grandeur. No wonder that it is a sacred mountain, and so dear to the Japanese that their art is never weary of representing it. It was nearly fifty miles off when we first saw it."[9]

Photographs of the mountain abound. Relatively close to the port of Yokohama, Mount Fuji and nearby Lake Hakone were readily accessible to Western travelers. Furthermore, the dormant volcano, as Bird noted, was well known in the West, primarily through Katsushika Hokusai's woodblock prints, which had been available in Europe since the 1860s. In order to capitalize on these accepted visions of the mountain, photographers such as Tamamura Kozaburō often quoted directly from the prints. For example, a comparison between Tamamura's *Mount Fuji from Numazu* (plate 34) with Hokusai's *The Surface of the Water at Misaka in Kai Province* from the series "Thirty-six Views of Mount Fuji" reveals that Tamamura adopted the woodblock print artist's juxtaposition of the distant mountain with the watery foreground, as well as his effective exploitation of the cone-shaped reflection.

Similarly, photographs of Tokyo (known before the Meiji era as Edo) frequently took their lead from earlier painted and printed images. Sites such as Ueno Park and Mukōjima (along the Sumida River) that were home to many a boisterous cherry blossom viewing party, and the Yoshiwara brothel district had been depicted as scenic places within the burgeoning metropolis since the late seventeenth century. The temple precincts of Asakusa Sensōji, described by nineteenth-century tourists as the home of "one of the most famous of the thirty-three famous Kwannons [*sic*] of the empire, the great place of worship for the masses, and the centre of a Vanity Fair unequalled elsewhere,"[10] were the subject of countless images, including one in Utagawa Hiroshige's woodblock print series "Famous Places of Edo" (*Meisho Edo hyakkei*). Hiroshige's selection and depiction of scenic places of Edo were reflected in many of the most popular nineteenth-century photographs of Tokyo, including the Kameidō Tenjin Shrine and the Horikiri Iris Garden.

Also adopted in the photographs were the seasonal associations with individual locales that the earlier artists had emphasized; for example, Kusakabe Kimbei chose to photograph the autumn maple trees of the Takinogawa in Oji. So influential were these traditional relationships between place and season that even tourists who were in Japan for only a brief time purchased images from seasons that they could not possibly have enjoyed. The representation of the place with all its allusions took precedence over actual experience.

THE CREATION OF A NEW MEISHO TRADITION

Two of the most widely photographed sites in Japan in the nineteenth century were the thirteenth-century Great Buddha (*Daibutsu*) in Kamakura and the seventeenth-century mausoleums of the Tokugawa shoguns Ieyasu and Iemitsu in Nikkō (called Tōshōgū). Described in the guidebooks as "stand[ing] alone among Japanese works of art," the Great Buddha was seen as embodying "the spiritual peace which comes of perfected knowledge and the subjugation of all passion."[11] Despite the esteem that the forty-nine- foot image elicited among nineteenth-century tourists, the statue located in the sleepy backwater of Kamakura had never been considered as a traditional *meisho*. In fact, the colossal bronze did not achieve fame until the latter part of the nineteenth century, when Felice Beato photographed it.[12] His images, dating to about 1864, depict the Buddha from the front with men standing nearby to establish scale. Similar images by later photographers must have been extensively circulated, for the artist John La Farge wrote about the statue in his *An Artist's Letters from Japan*: "The photographs must long have made you know it."[13]

Foreign tourists picked up a Japanese aphorism: "He who has not seen Nikko [*sic*] must not use the word kek'ko [splendid, delicious, beautiful]."[14] Although in the Edo period generations of Tokugawa rulers and their entourages were obliged to make pilgrimages and pay homage to their ancestors, traditionally, access to the shrines and the individual mausoleums had largely been proscribed for commoners.[15] After the Meiji Restoration of 1868 and the overthrow of the Tokugawa regime, however, general access became possible, and photographs made the site familiar to a wider audience. Surprisingly, foreigners were some of the earliest

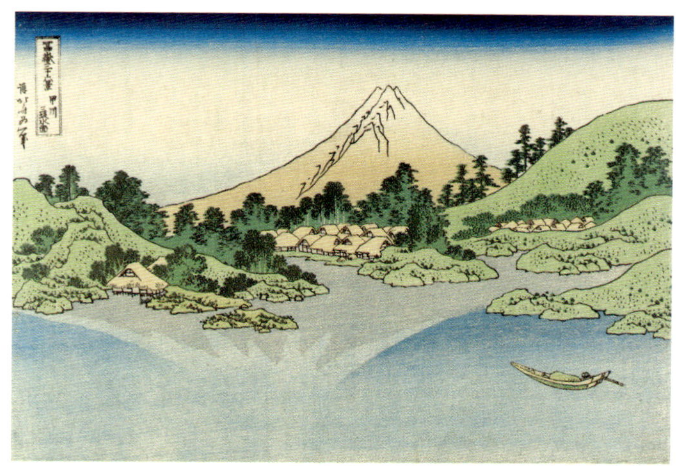

Katsushika Hokusai, The surface of the water at Misaka *(about 1830)*

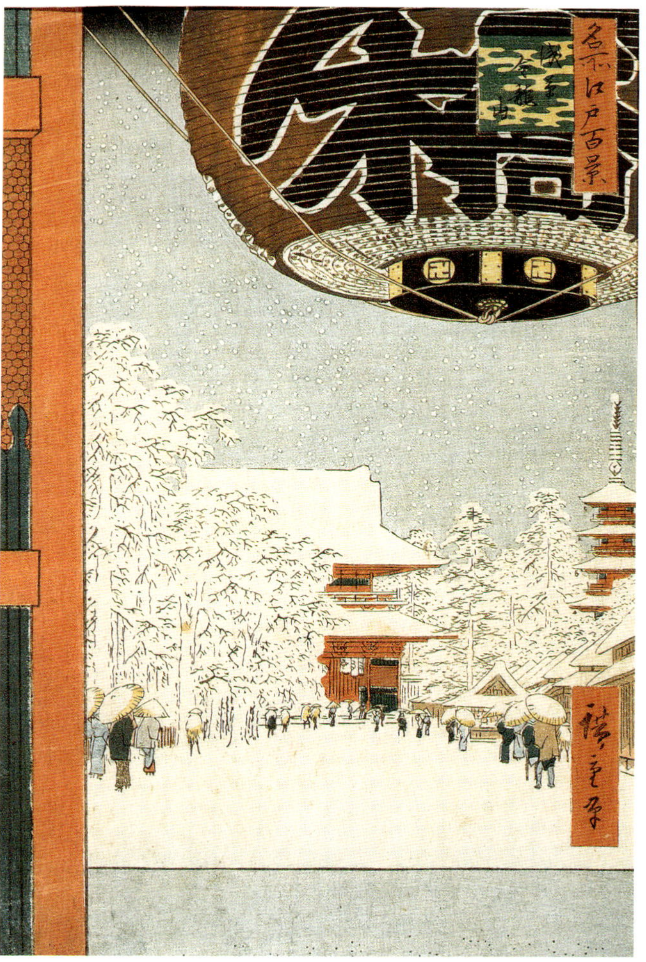

Utagawa Hiroshige, The Kinryūzan Temple at Asakusa *(1856)*

tourists there. In 1870, contemporary journals relate that Sir Harry Parkes, head of the British Legation in Japan, and his wife were the first foreigners to whom the shrine grounds were fully revealed "to wonder and admiration."[16] With the notable exception of the scientific ethicist Albert Leffingwell, who traveled to Japan in the late 1880s and who found the shrines to be excessive, most visitors marveled at the opulently ornamented shrines and the towering cryptomeria trees that lined its avenues, and most wanted to take photographs of Nikkō home with them. Of the numerous structures in the complex, the most widely photographed were the Yōmeimon, the gate with elaborate white columns supporting capitals of mythical beasts and friezes of Chinese immortals that marked the entrance to the inner precinct, and Ieyasu's tomb in the form of a simple bronze pagoda.

It is worth noting that Edo-period painted images of the Tōshōgū complex were similarly limited. Seventeenth-century pilgrimage mandalas and festival screens provided only a bird's-eye view of the shrine.[17] It seems likely that it was foreign photographers, men such as Felice Beato, Baron Raimund von Stillfried-Ratenicz, and Adolfo Farsari, who were instrumental in establishing the visual markers by which Nikkō came to be known and which so appealed to foreigners with Victorian tastes and an admiration for Japanese craftsmanship.

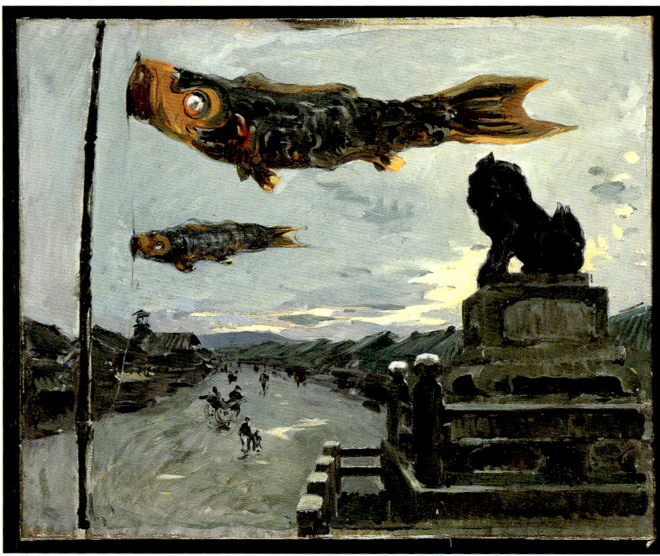

Louis Dumoulin, Carp Banners in Kyoto *(1888), many details of which were taken from Farsari's photograph of the same site*

PHOTOGRAPHS AS INTERMEDIARIES OF AUTHENTICITY

As numerous nineteenth-century travel accounts indicate, photographs created impressions about Japan and its attractions long before tourists arrived on its shores. Upon disembarking — with guidebooks and in some cases, photo albums, already in hand — foreign visitors set out to experience the country described by the romantic images they already knew.[18] For some, as is the case with many a modern tourist, the temples, shrines, and scenic spots lost their individuality, but so long as the traveler secured photographs of a site the encounter could be considered authentic.

One photograph could be substituted for another, or a photograph could even stand in the place of the travel experience itself. The degree to which photographs mediated the experience of tourists is illustrated by *View of a monumental bell at Hōkōji* (plate 2) by an unidentified artist. Albert Leffingwell, who purchased it, subsequently had an engraved rendition produced to accompany his 1892 travel account, *Rambles through Japan without a Guide*. The print illustrates his description of a bell near the grounds of a Kyoto temple: "fourteen feet high, nine feet in diameter, and a weight of over sixty-three tons, dimensions rarely exceeded even in the largest bells of Europe."[19] In this way, Leffingwell appropriated a generic photograph of a bell for a document of his own personal experience.

A canvas by the French painter Louis Dumoulin, who traveled to Asia in 1888 and 1889, conflates a site in Yokohama with a photograph of a Kyoto site. Dumoulin borrowed the particulars of his painting from the Kyoto photograph by Farsari (plate 37). The stone guardian lion in Farsari's foreground juxtaposed with the broad avenue of wooden houses would have been immediately recognizable to the Japanese as a depiction of Shijō, one of the main thoroughfares in Kyoto. In the 1889 catalogue for an exhibition of the paintings resulting from his journey, however, Dumoulin described the oil as depicting the Boys' Festival viewed from the Bluff in Yokohama.[20] Evidently Dumoulin (who may not have even traveled to Kyoto) had internalized the photograph and it, not the actual site, had become the painter's experience.

As John La Farge noted about travel in Japan, "The general memory is impressive and grand; the details run one into the other."[21] Photographs provided Western tourists with a powerful means for reconstructing their travels; traditional imagery produced by a new technology enabled them to see "Old Japan" even in scenes of the "New Japan." Clearly many Western tourists were less concerned with the specifics of the places portrayed in photographs that they brought home with them than with the idea of Japan that these images confirmed.

1. The Englishman Basil Chamberlain relayed this description of Japan in a speech by his compatriot Sir Edwin Arnold in *Things Japanese: Being Notes on Various Subjects Connected with Japan for the Use of Travelers and Others*, fifth edition revised (London: John Murray, 1905), 3.

2. Anne Nishimura Morse, "At the Intersection of 'Old Japan' and 'New Japan': The Museum of Fine Arts, Boston, and the Meiji Era" in *Japan at the Dawn of the Modern Age* (Boston: MFA Publications, 2001), 13–22; and Christopher Benfey, *The Great Wave: Gilded Age Misfits, Japanese Eccentrics, and the Opening of Old Japan* (New York: Random House, 2003).

3. Chino Kaori, "Meisho e no seiritsu to tenkai," *Meisho-e*, vol. 10 of *Nihon byōbu-e shūsei* (Tokyo: Kōdansha, 1980), 115–121. For a brief comment in English see Louisa Cunningham, *The Spirit of Place* (New Haven: Yale University Art Gallery, 1984), 7–12.

4. Reproduced in Ozawa Kenji, ed., *Shashin de miru Bakumatsu Meiji* (Tokyo: Sekaibunkasha, 2000), 100. According to William Burto, "The cup of tea that cheers but not inebriates" is a quotation from the nineteenth-century English poet William Cowper.

5. Helen McCullough, trans., *Tales of Ise* (Stanford, Calif.: Stanford University Press, 1968), 130–31.

6. Eliza Ruhamah Scidmore, *Jinrikisha Days in Japan* (New York: Harper & Brothers, 1891), 343.

7. Basil Hall Chamberlain and W. B. Mason, *Handbook for Travellers in Japan Including the Whole Empire from Yezo to Formosa* (London: John Murray, 1901), 316.

8. For an excellent discussion of the political interpretation of the iconography of *rakuchū rakugai* painting, see Matthew P. McKelway, "The Partisan View: Rakuchū Rakugai Screens in the Mary and Jackson Burke Collection," *Orientations*, v. 28, no. 2 (February 1997): 48–57.

9. Isabella Bird, *Unbeaten Tracks: An Account of Travels on Horseback in the Interior Including Visits to the Aborigines of Yezo and the Shrines of Nikko and Ise*, vol. 1 (New York: G. P. Putnam's Sons, 1881), 13–14.

10. Scidmore, *Jinrikisha Days*, 52.

11. Chamberlain and Mason, *Handbook for Travellers in Japan*, 102.

12. The author would like to express her appreciation to Allen Hockley for having pointed out Beato's contribution. Beato's images are reproduced in Ozawa, ed., *Shashin de miru Bakumatsu Meiji*, 58; and Terry Bennett, *Early Japanese Images* (Rutland, Vt., and Tokyo: Charles E. Tuttle Company, 1996), 83.

13. John La Farge, *An Artist's Letters from Japan* (New York: Century Company, 1897), 225. La Farge goes on to describe that in 1886 he himself "took many photographs from new points of view," which are reflected in his watercolor *The Great Statue of Amida Buddha at Kamakura, Known as the Daibutsu, from the Priest's Garden* now in the collection of The Metropolitan Museum of Art, New York; see La Farge, 226. The watercolor is reproduced in Carnegie Museum of Art, Pittsburgh, and National Museum of American Art, Smithsonian Institution, eds., *John La Farge* (New York: Abbeville Press, 1987), 51.

14. Bird, *Unbeaten Tracks*, 84.

15. Constantine Nomikos Vaporis, *Breaking Barriers: Travel and the State in Early Modern Japan* (Cambridge, Mass., and London: Council on East Asian Studies, Harvard University, 1994), provides some details of the pilgrimages.

16. F. V. Dickins, *The Life of Sir Harry Parkes, K.C.B., G.C.M.G. Sometime her Majesty's Minister to China and Japan*, vol. 2 (London and New York: MacMillan, 1894), 162.

17. The *Nikkō Tōshōsha sankei zu byōbu* in a private collection, which records the appearance of the complex in 1636, and *Nikkō Tōshōsha sairei zu byōbu* in a private collection are published in Ibaragi Prefectural Museum, ed., *Tenkai sosho to Tōshō gongen* (Utsunomiya: Ibaragi Prefectural Museum, 1994), pls. 78 and 160.

18. See the essay by Frederic A. Sharf in this volume.

19. Albert Leffingwell, *Rambles through Japan without a Guide* (New York: The Baker and Taylor Company, 1892), 179–80.

20. *Exposition Louis Dumoulin: Tableaux et etudes de l'extrême-Orient: Japon, Chine-Cochinchine, Maslaisie* (Paris: Galleries Georges Petit, 1889), 2.

21. La Farge, *An Artist's Letters*, 233.

The Album

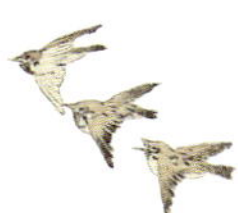

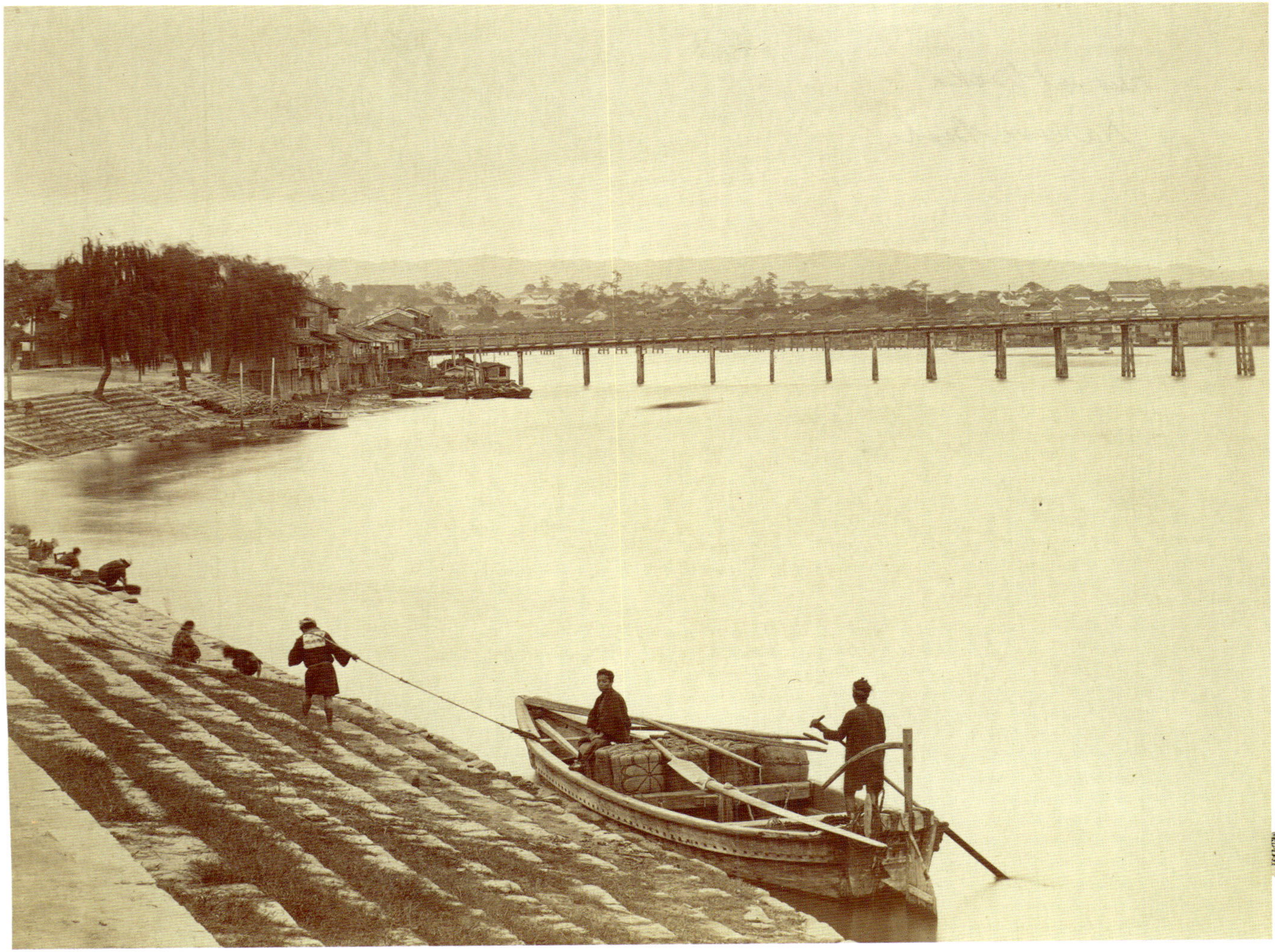

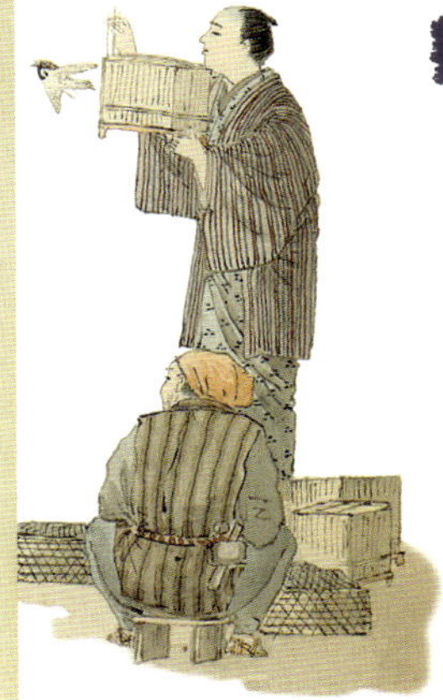

PLATE I

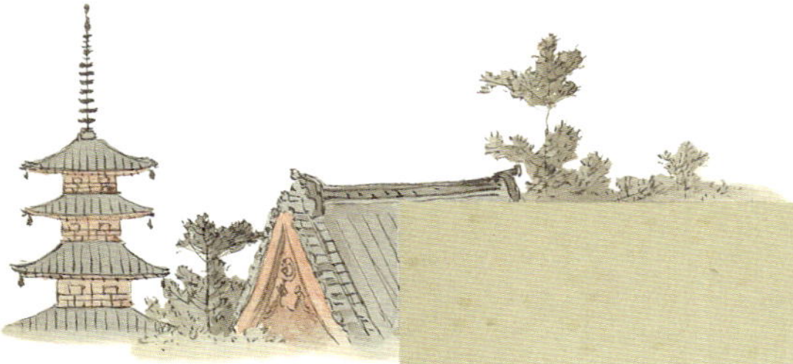

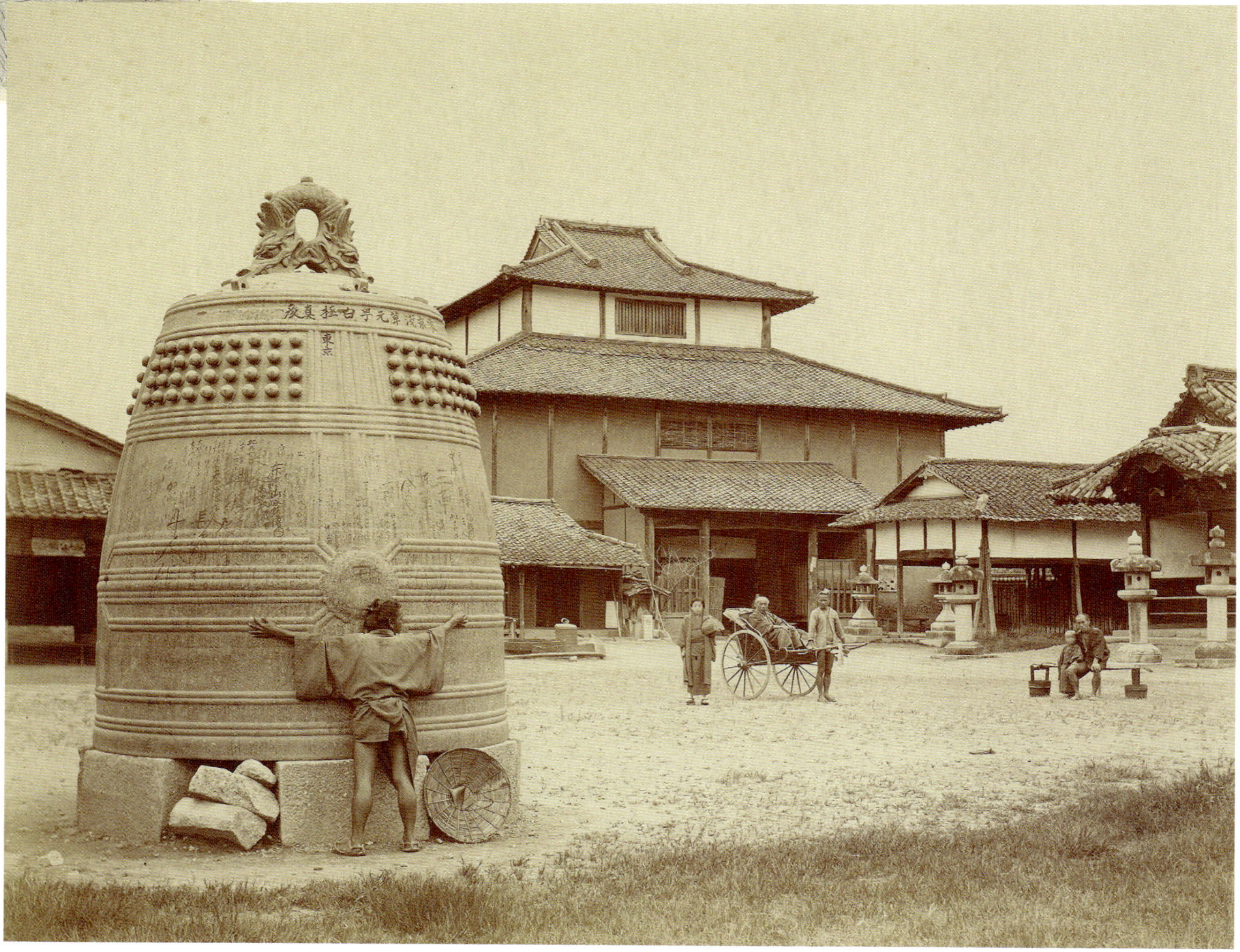

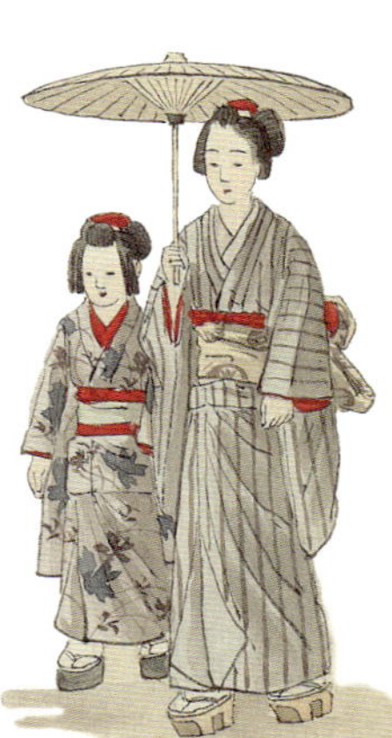

PLATE 2

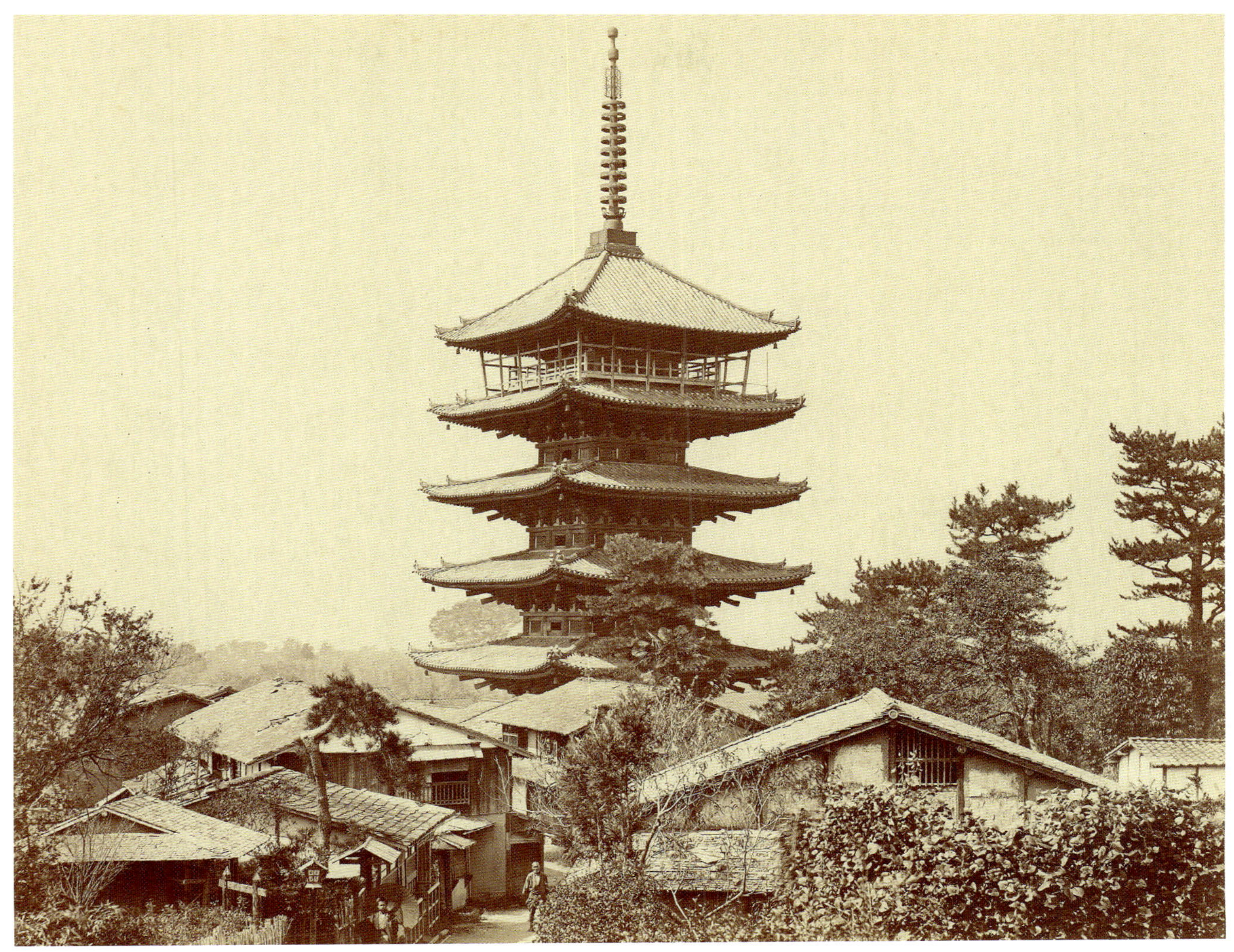

PLATE 3

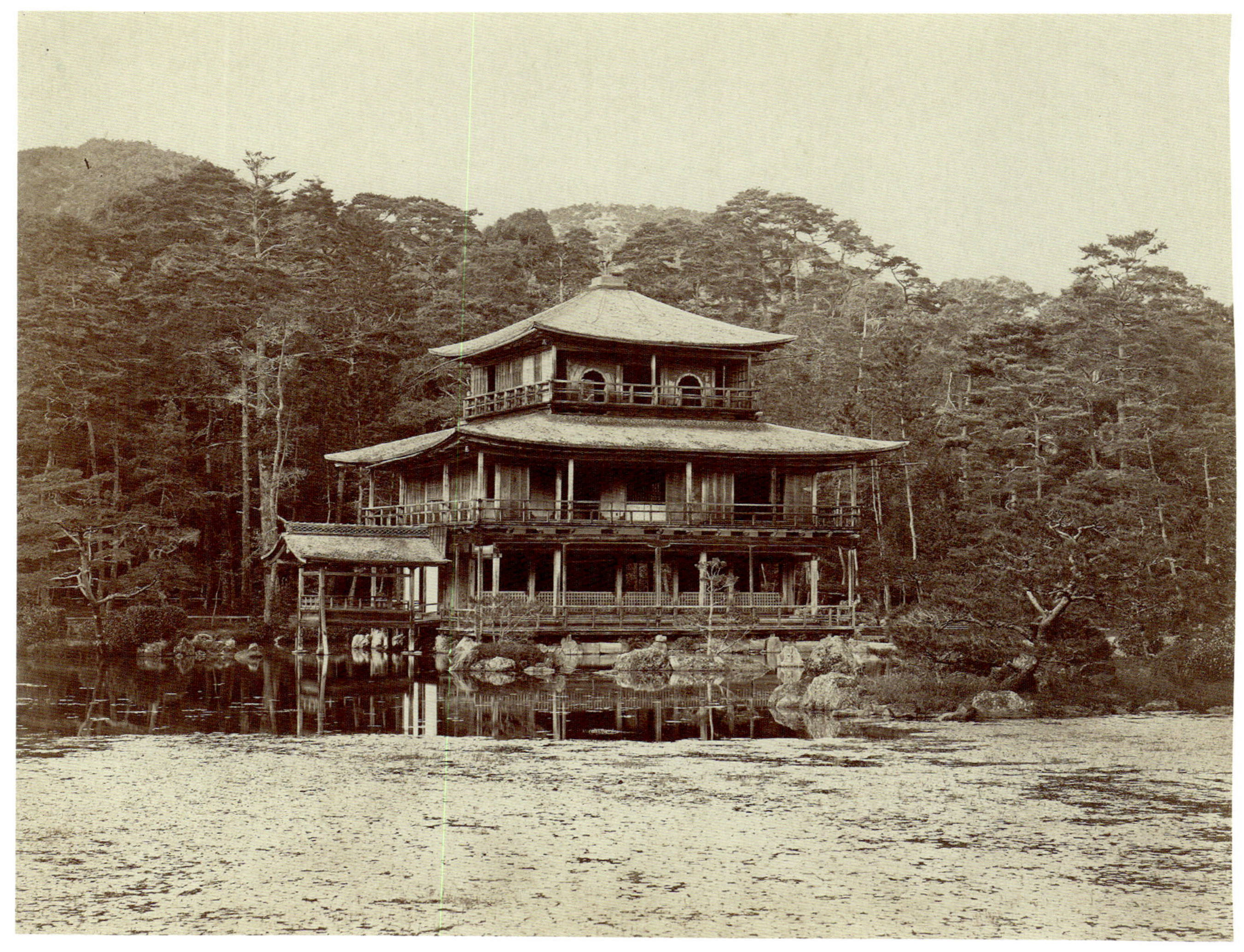

PLATE 4

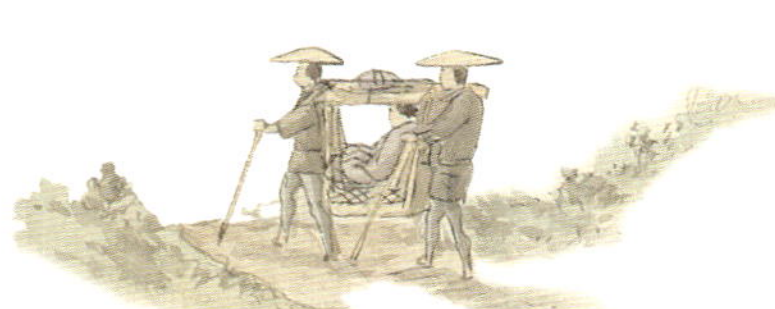

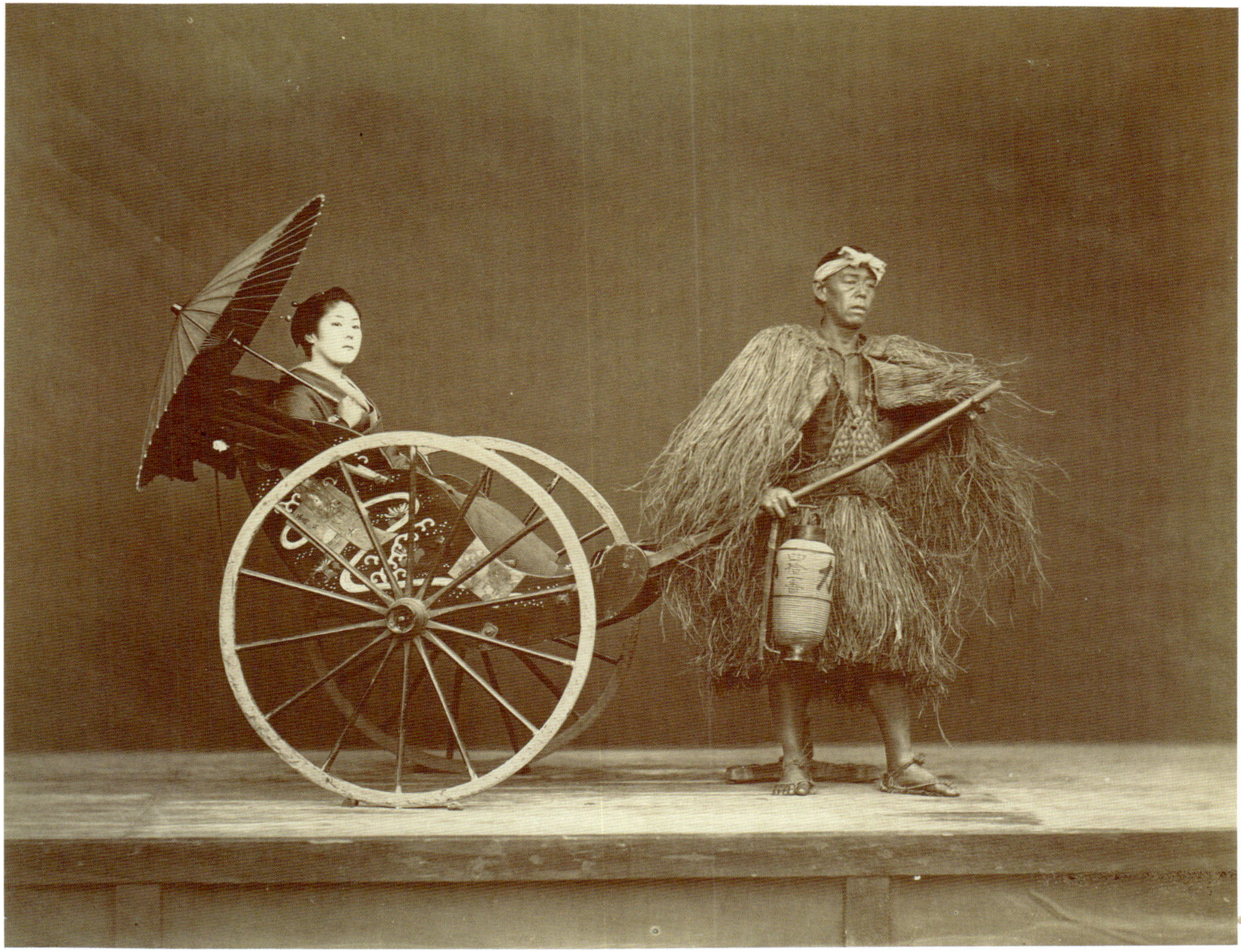

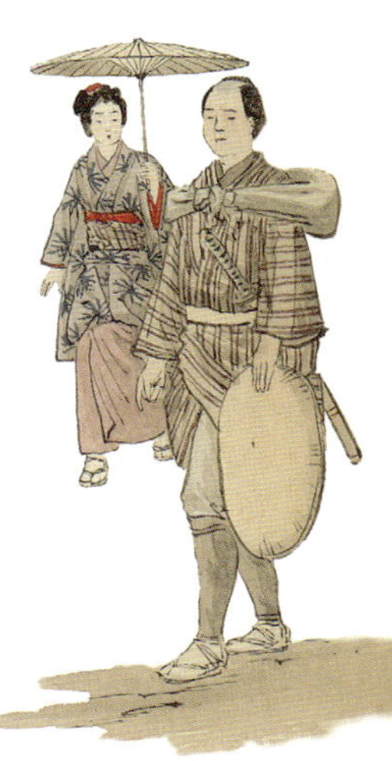

PLATE 5

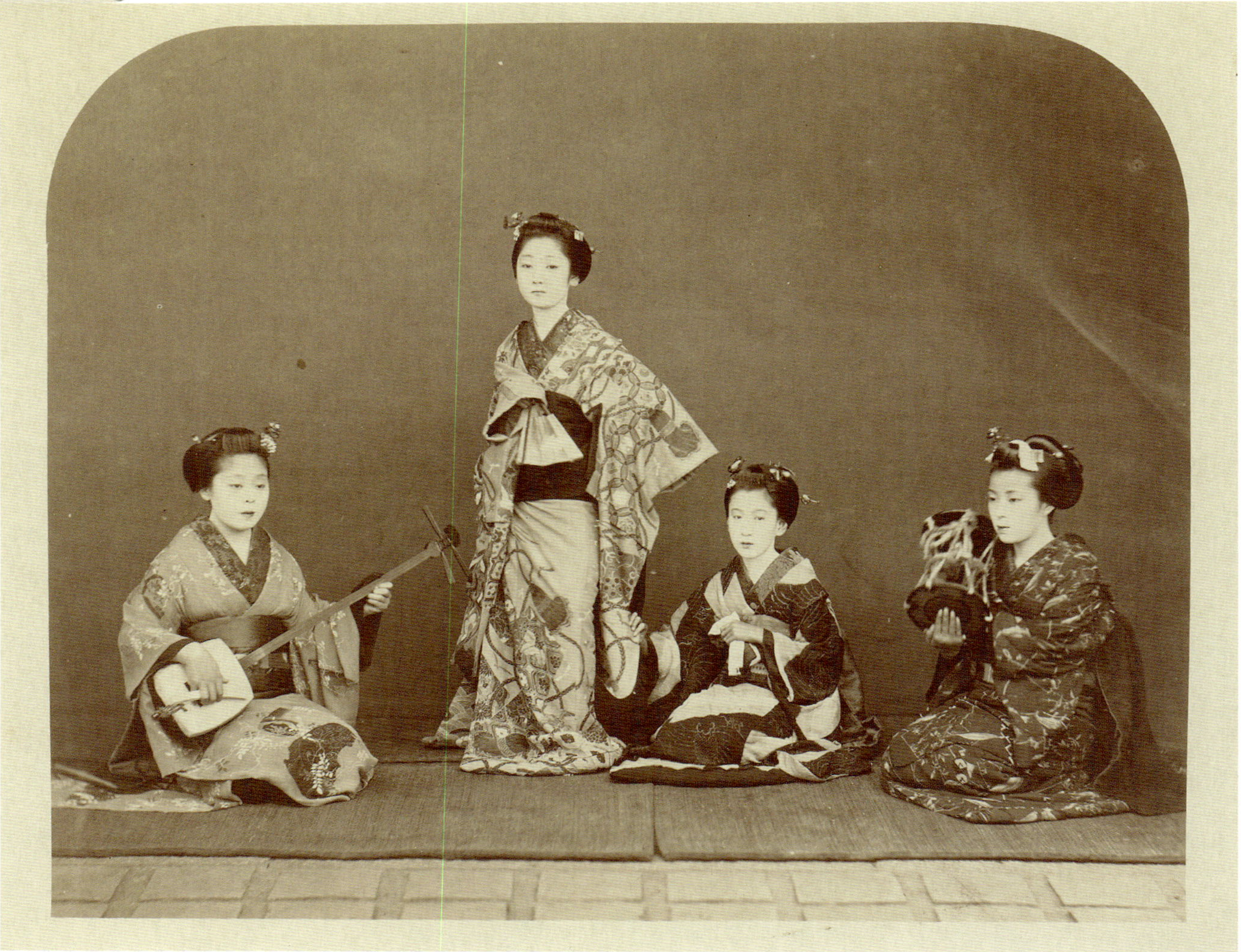

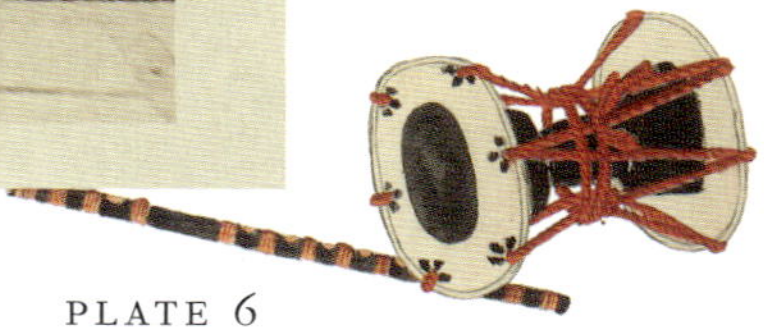

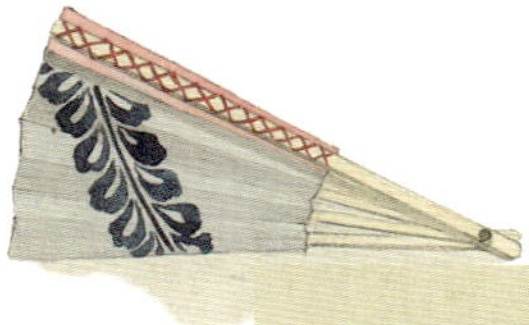

PLATE 6

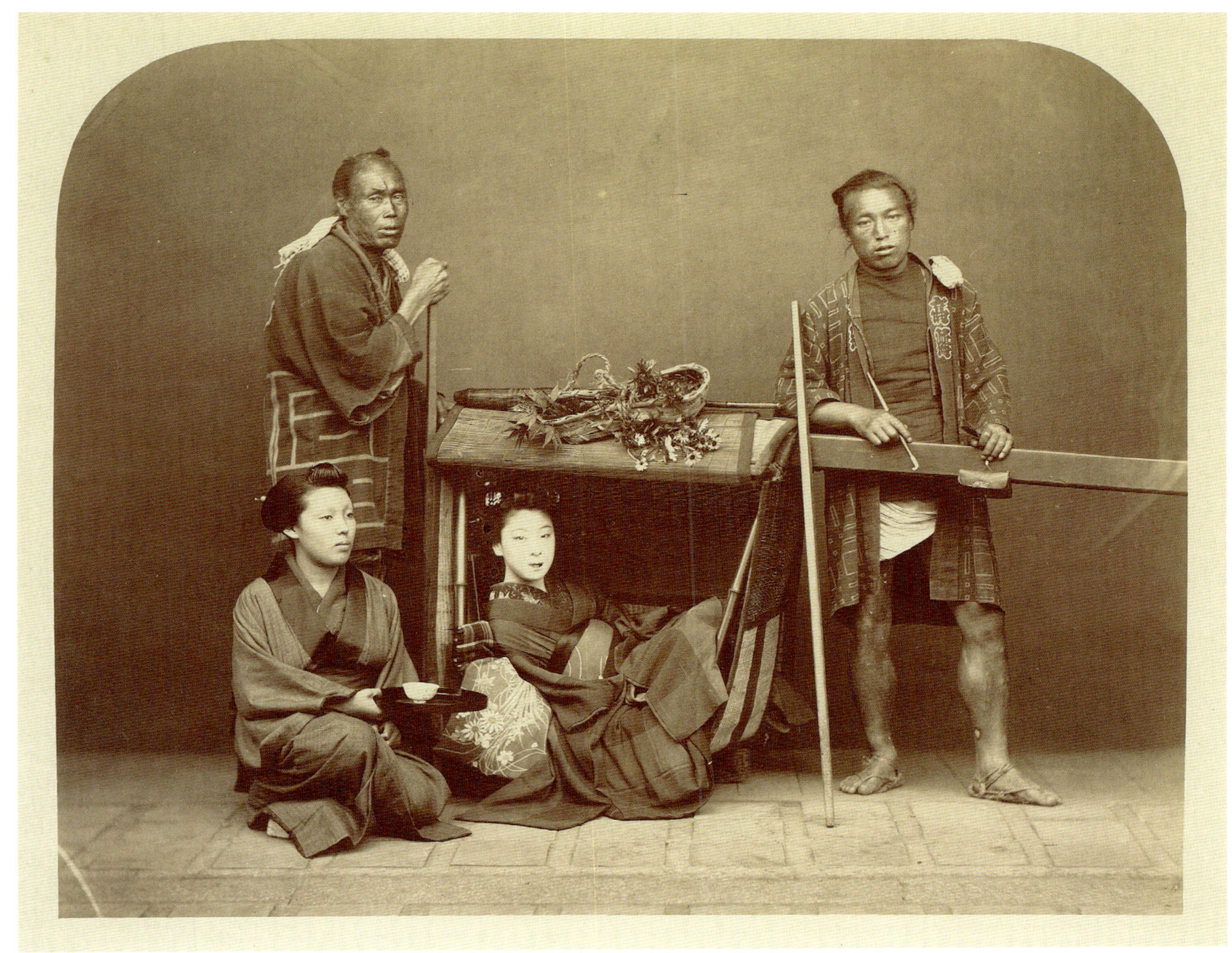

PLATE 7

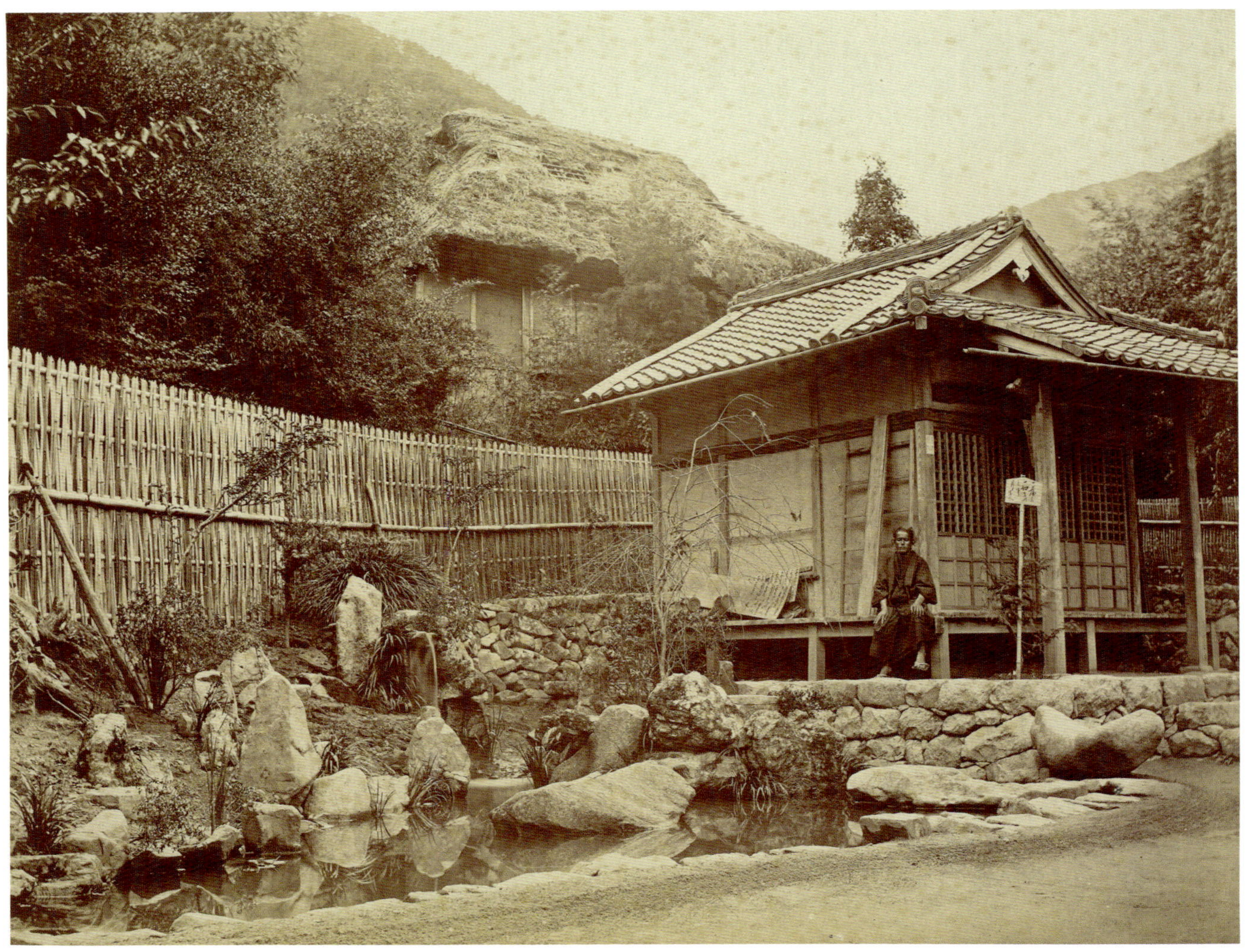

PLATE 8

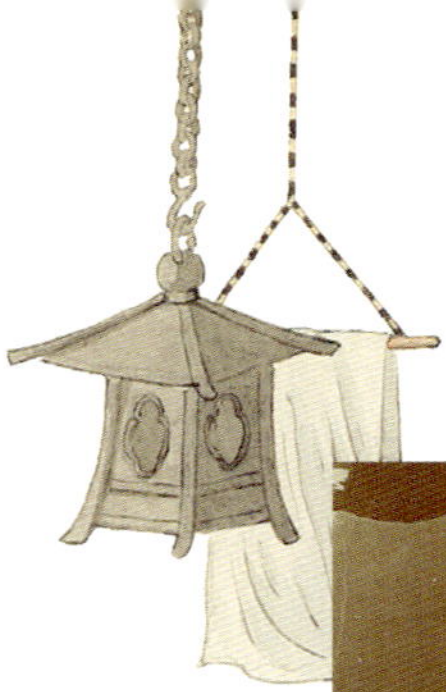

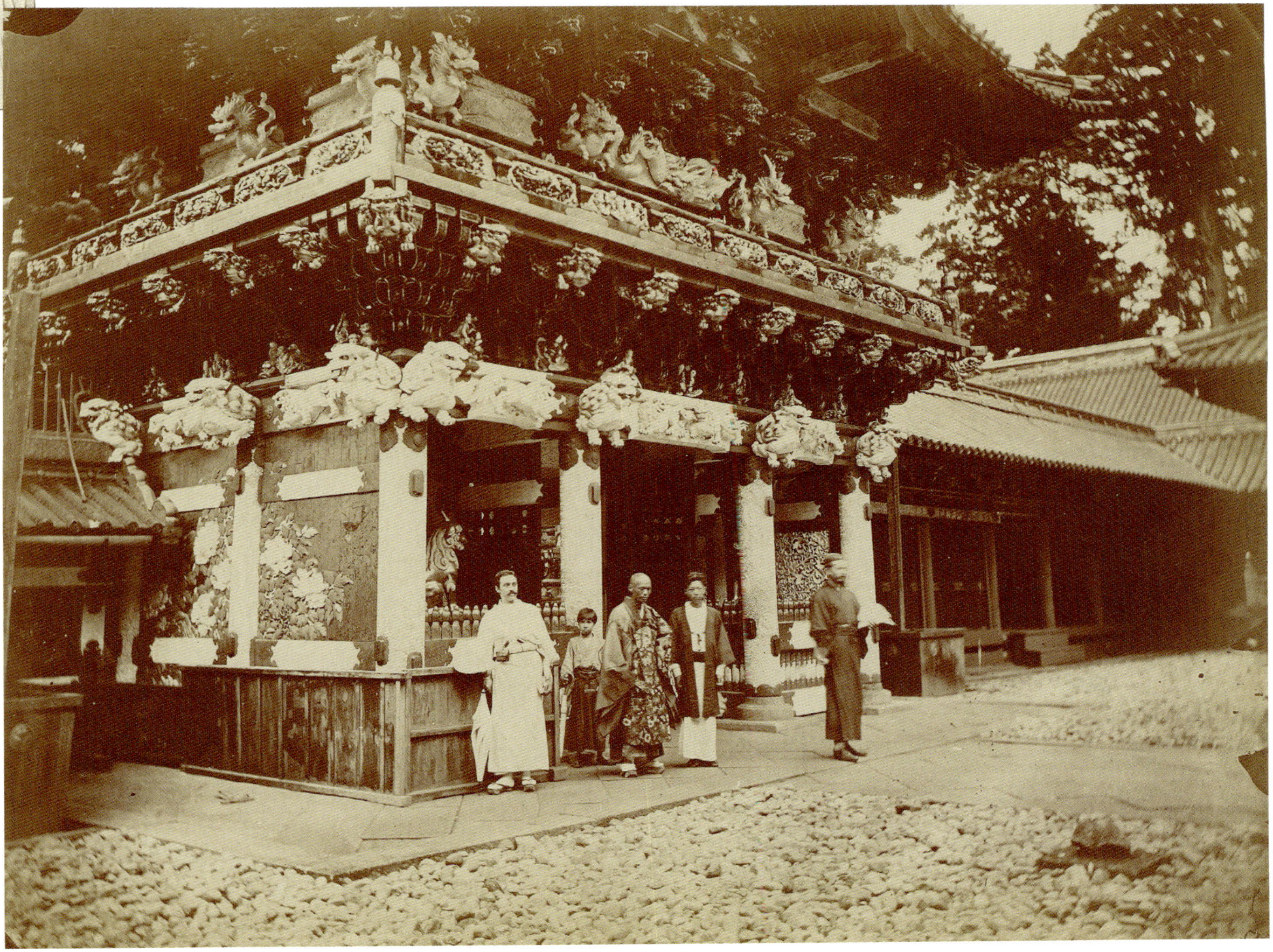

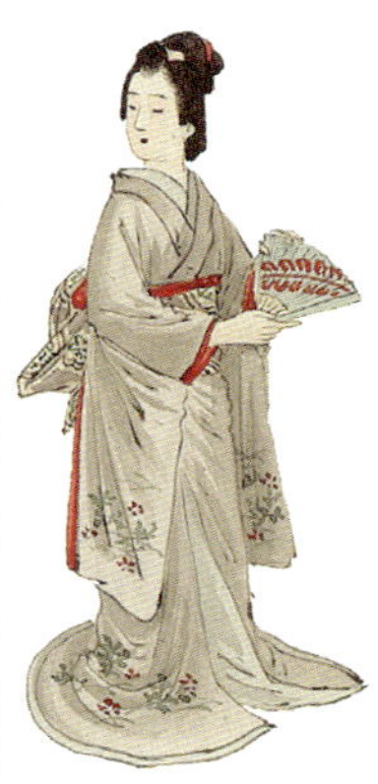

PLATE 9

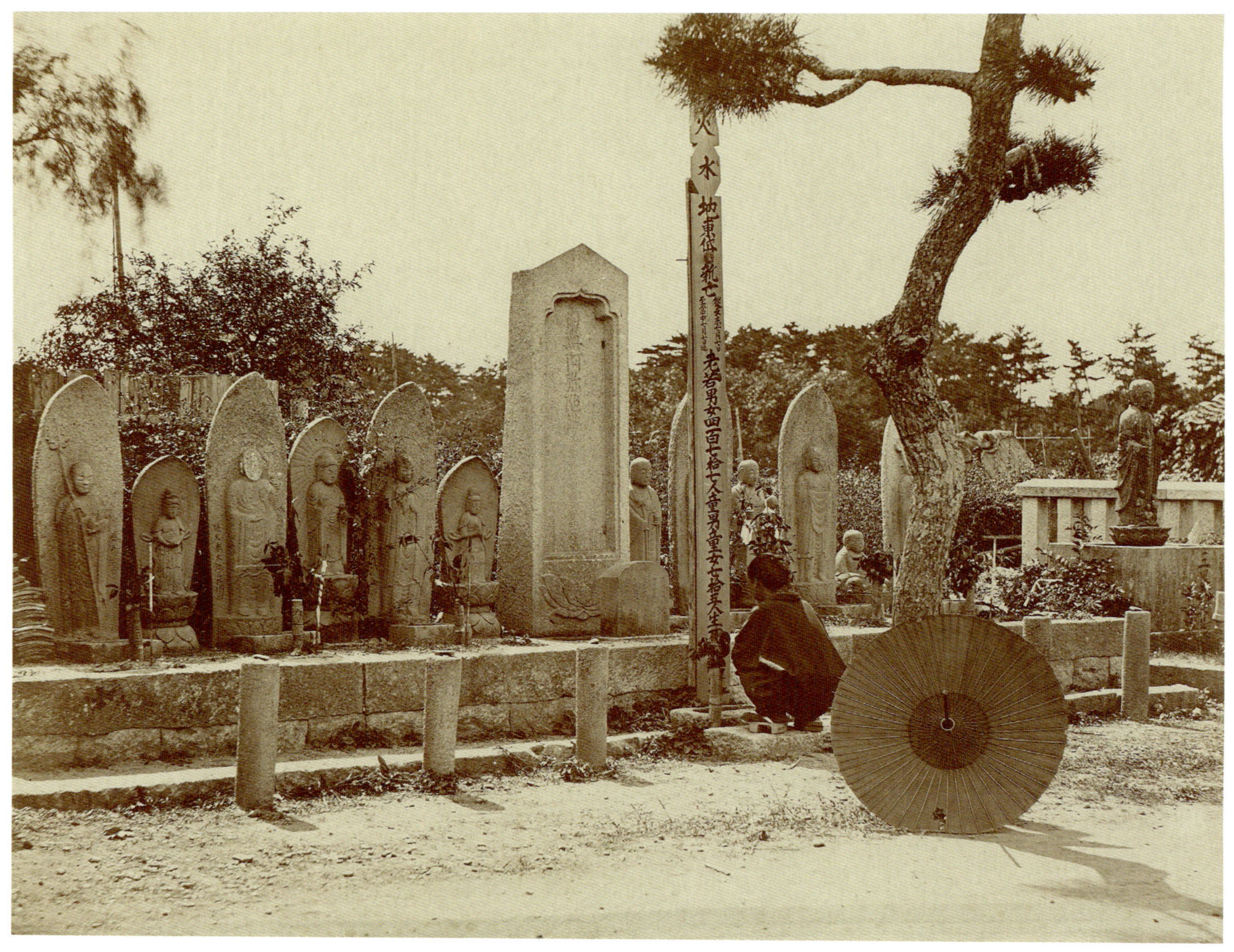

PLATE 10

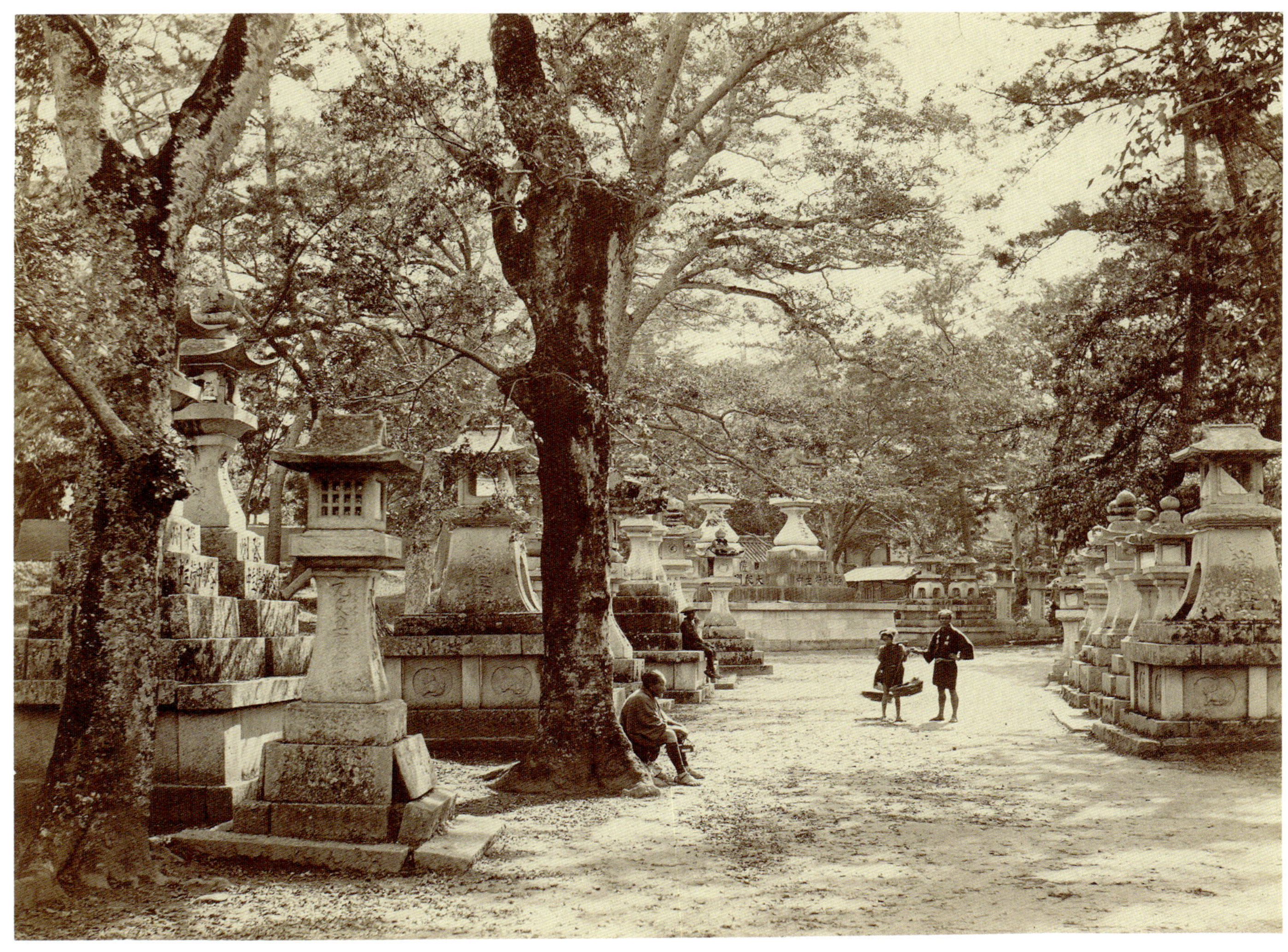

PLATE II

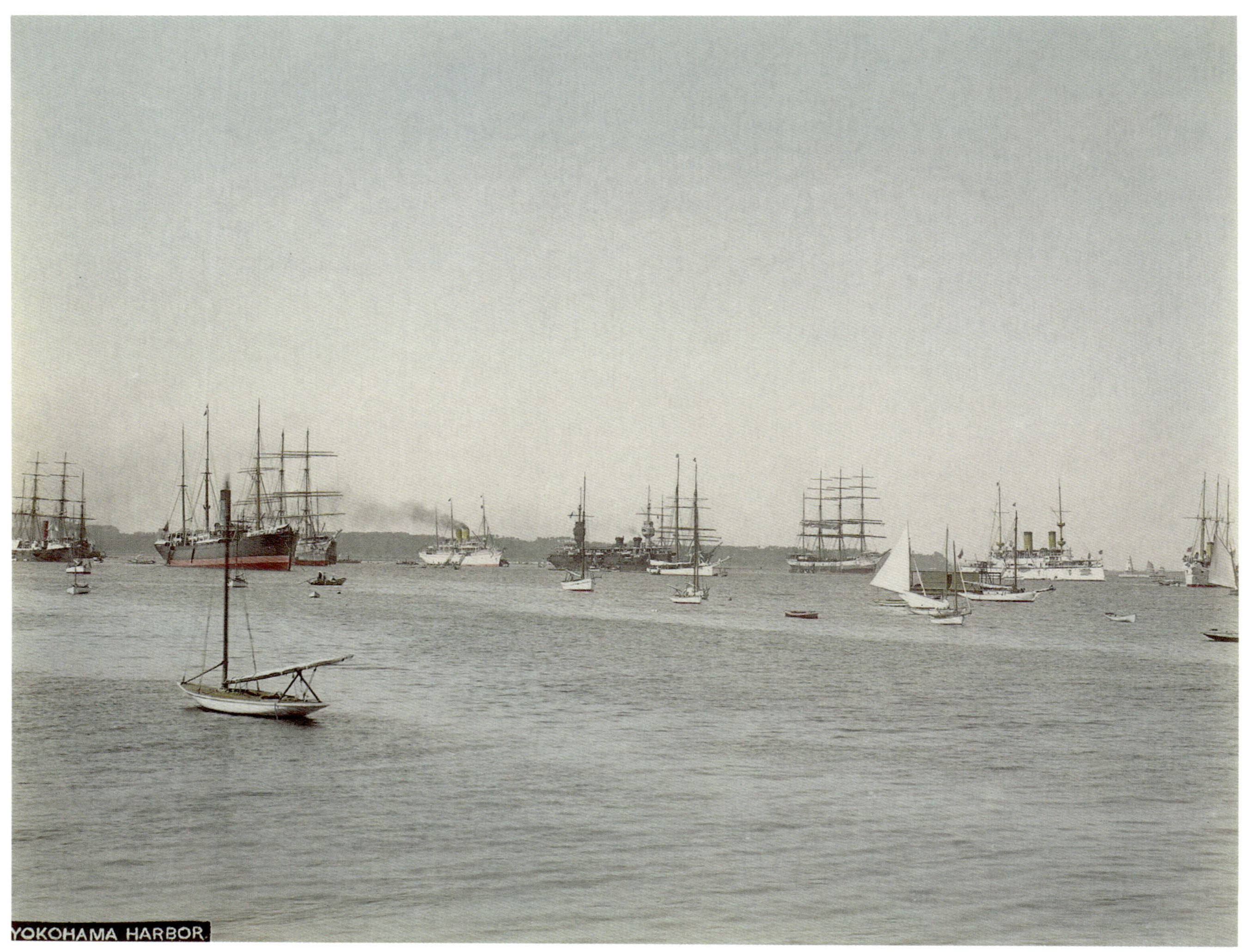

PLATE 12

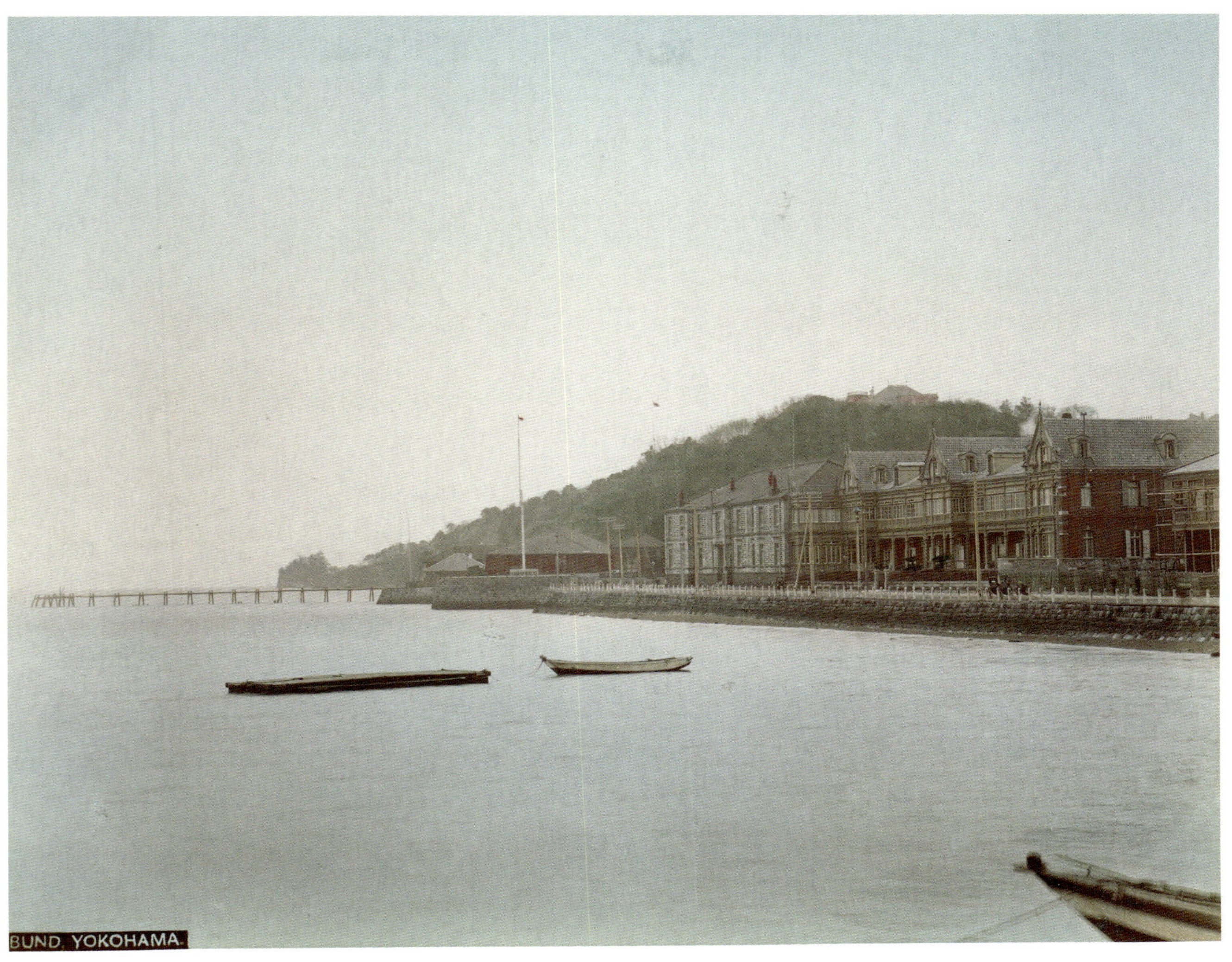

PLATE 13

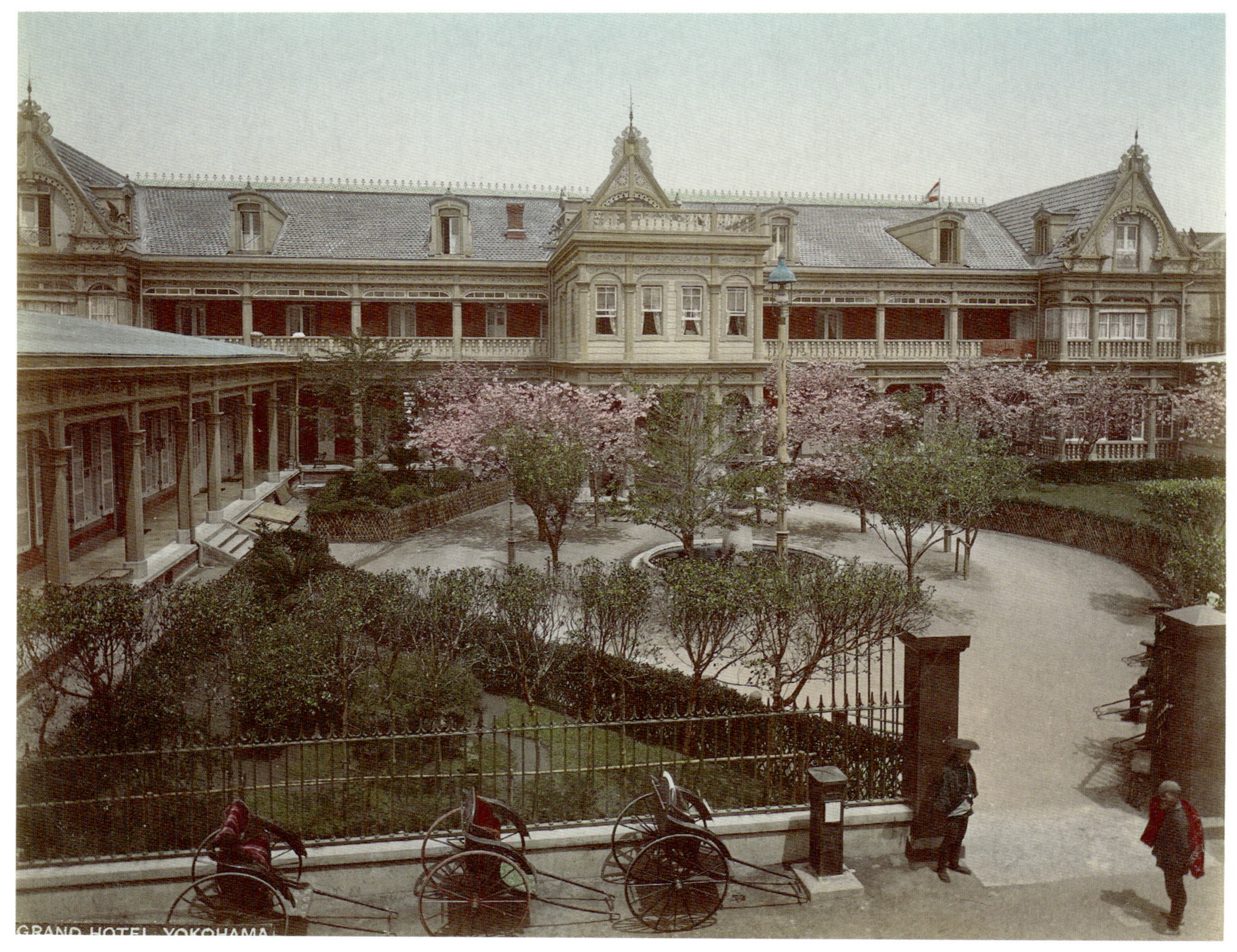

PLATE 14

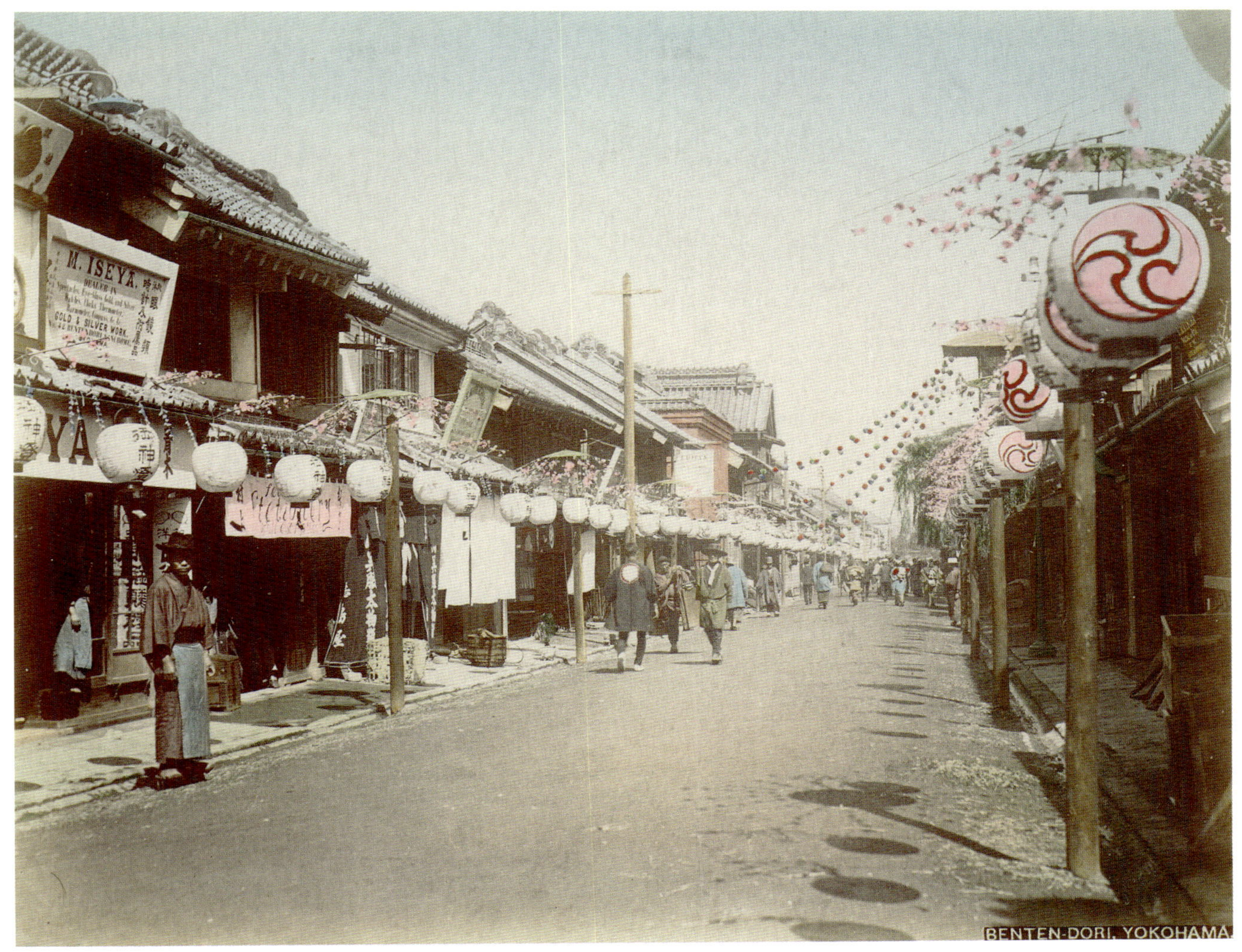

PLATE 15

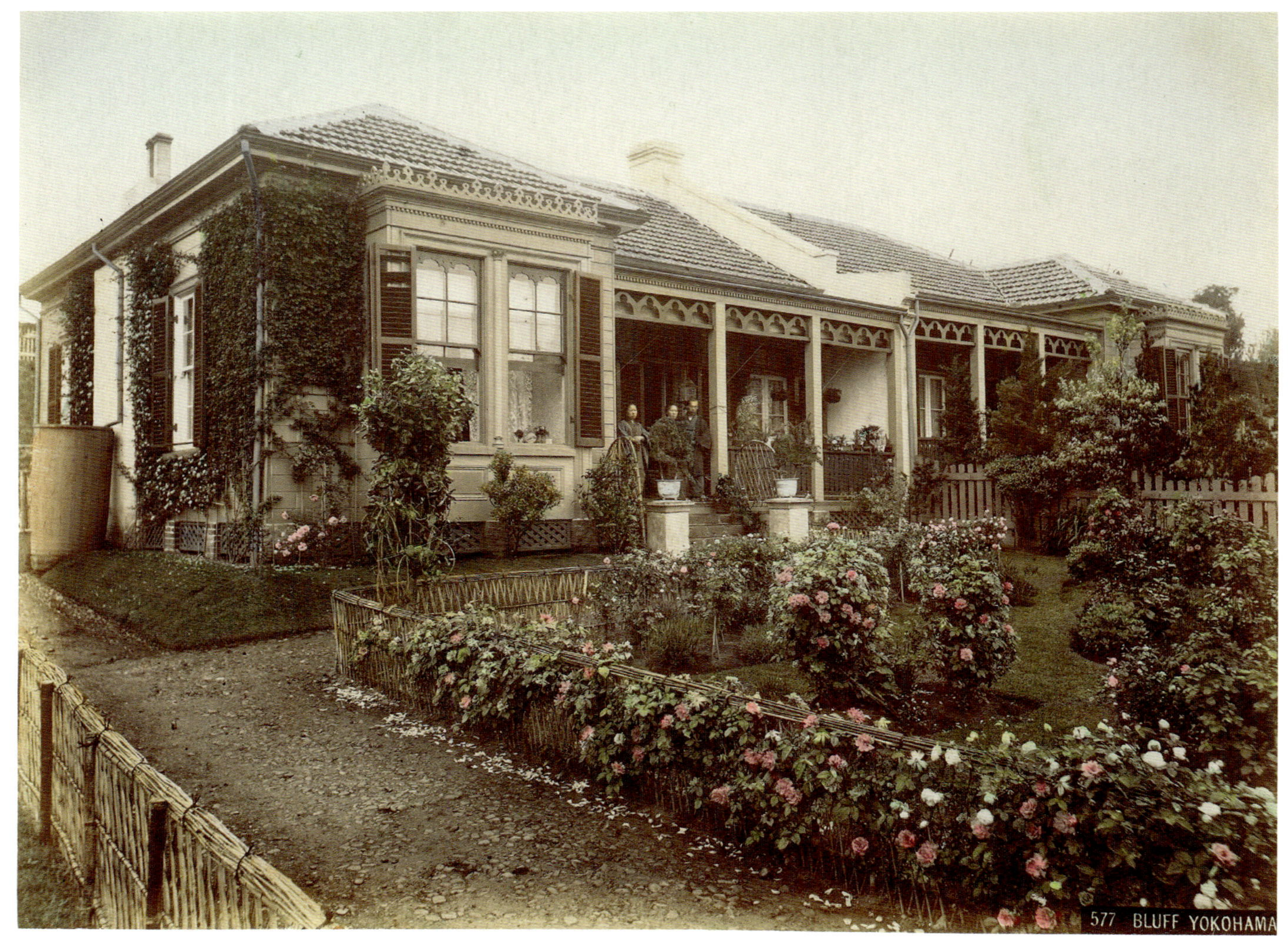

PLATE 16

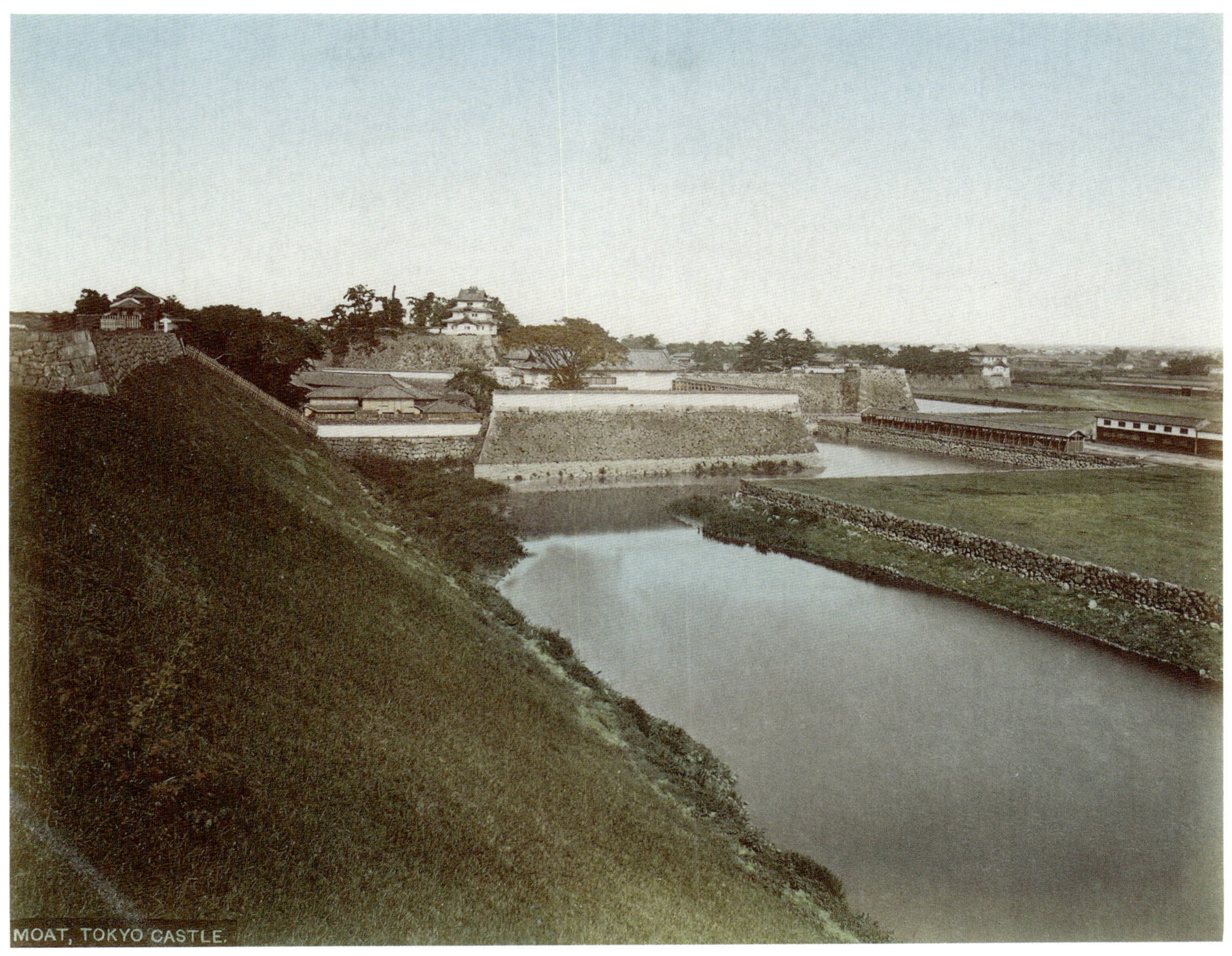

PLATE 17

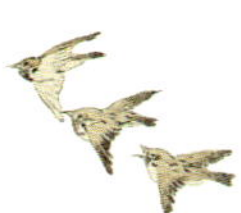

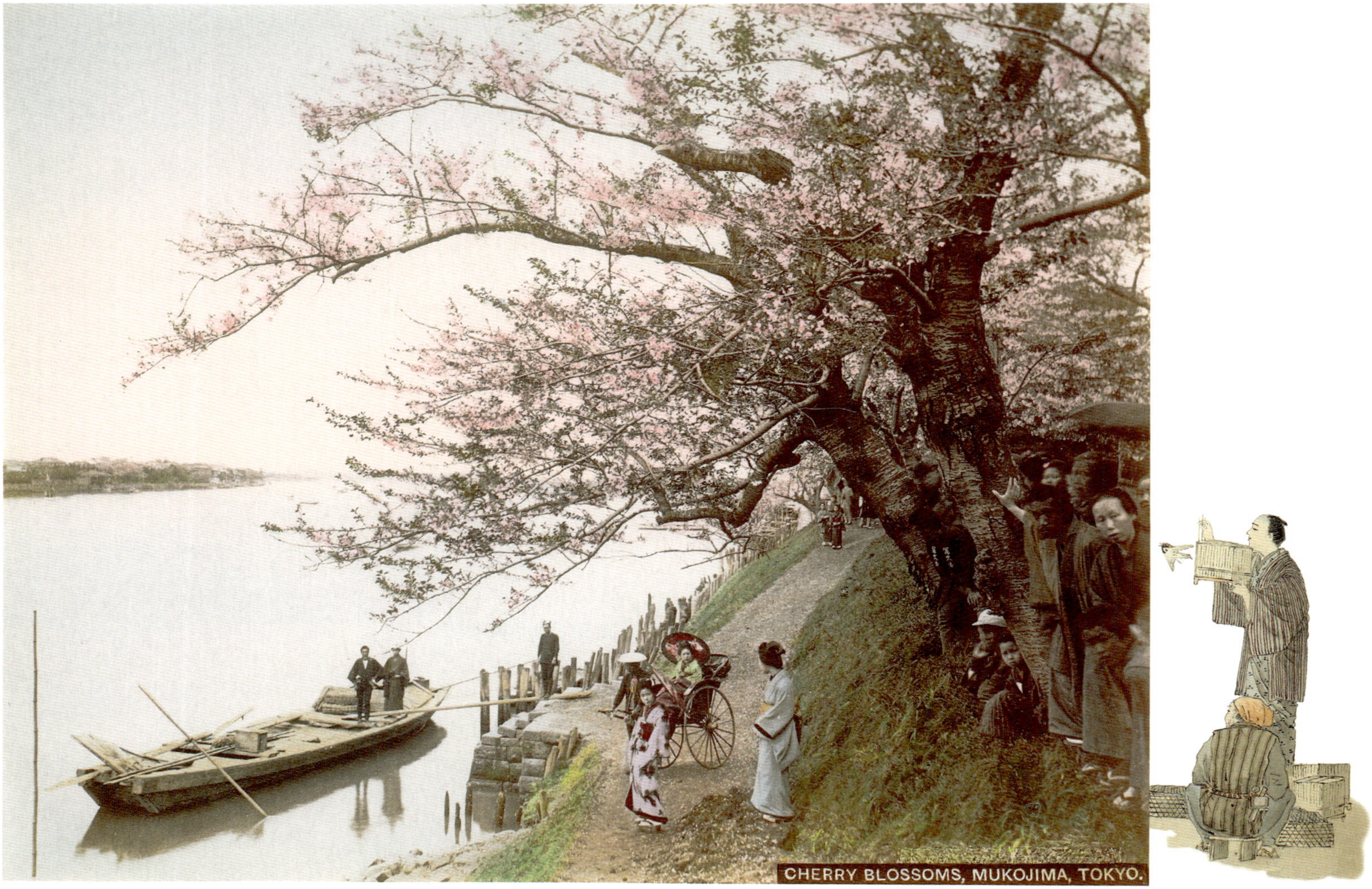

CHERRY BLOSSOMS, MUKOJIMA, TOKYO.

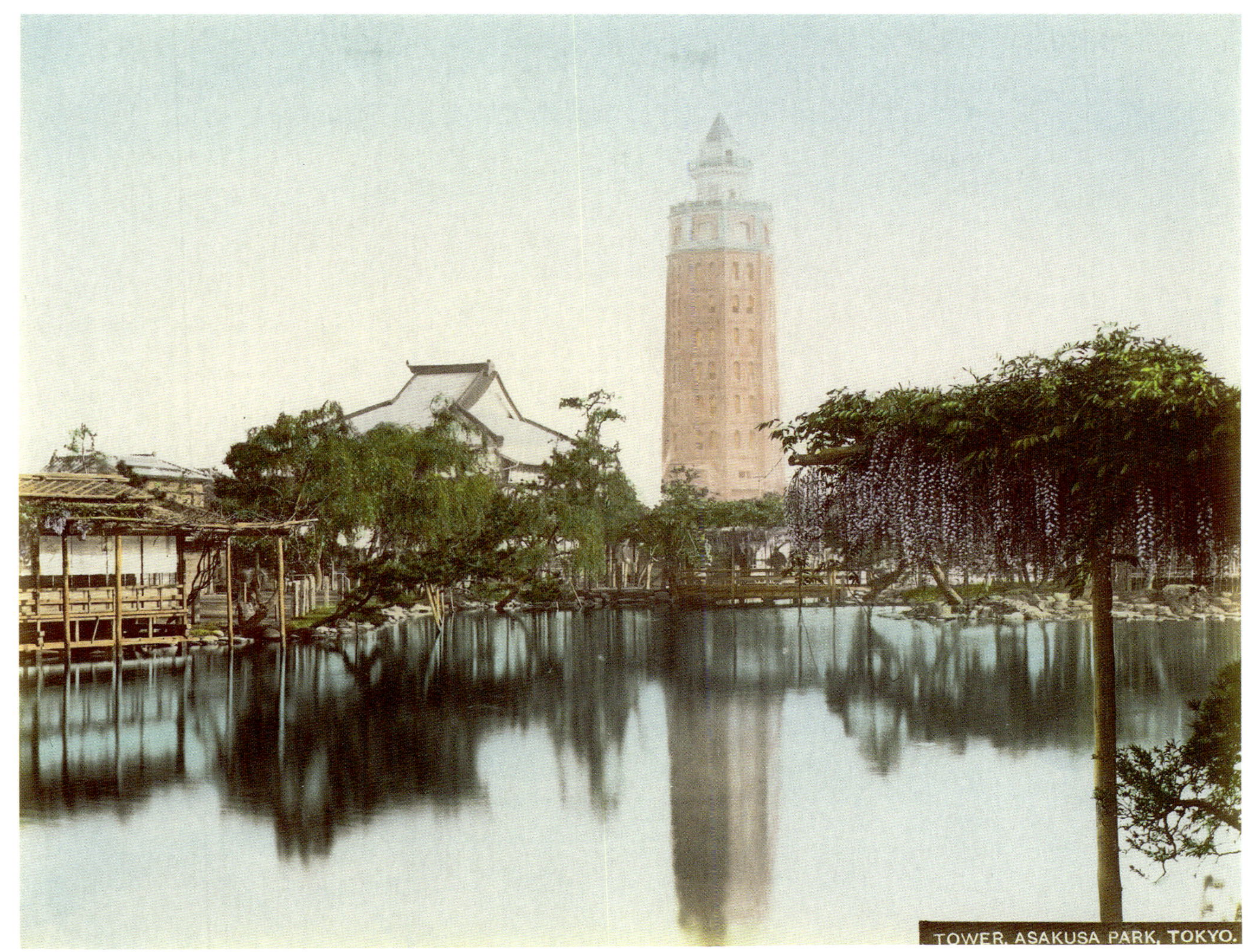

PLATE 19

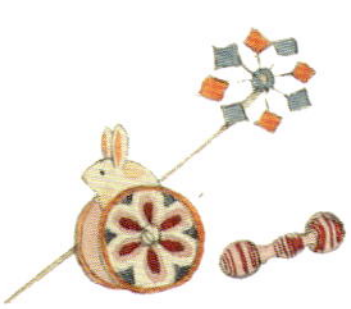

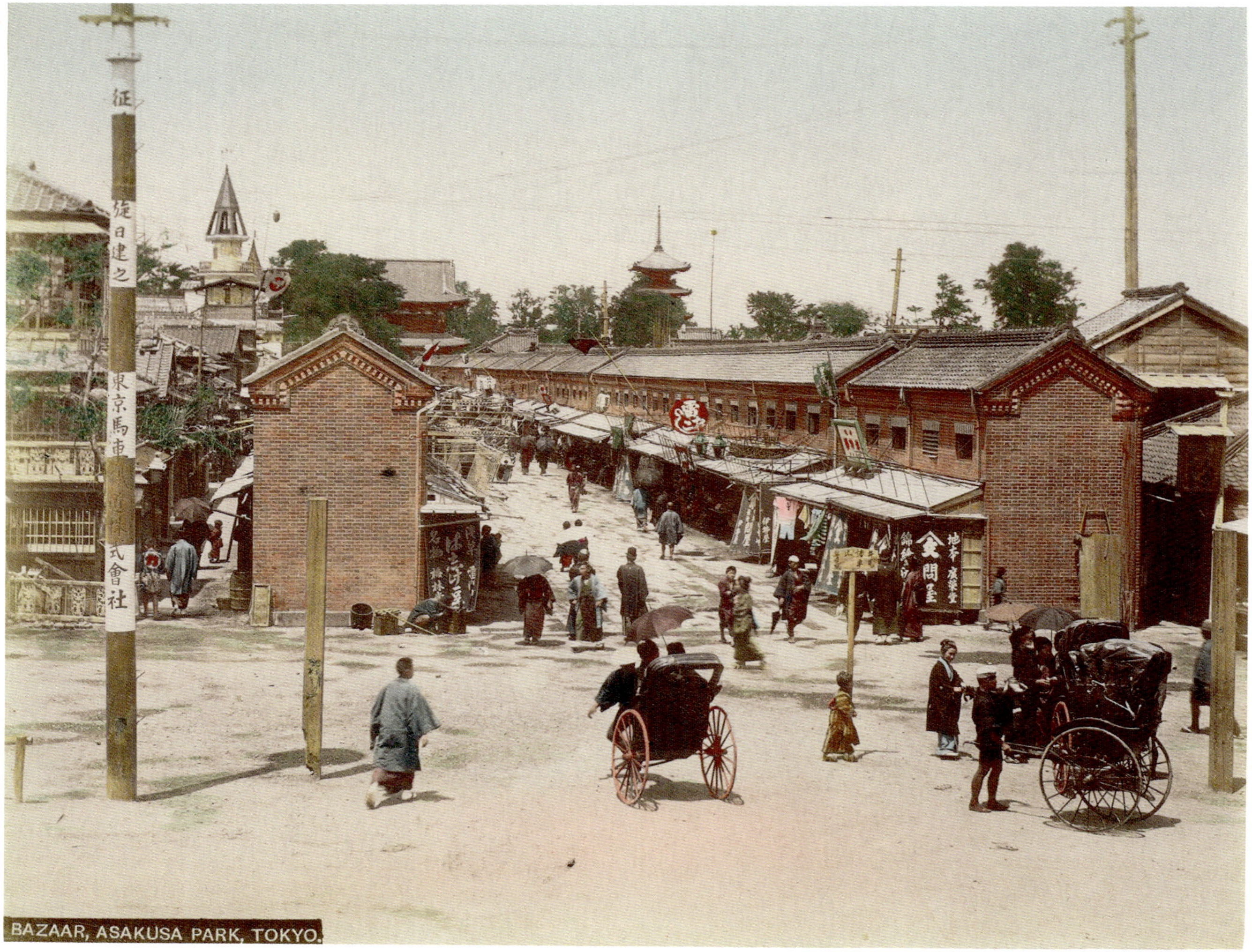

BAZAAR, ASAKUSA PARK, TOKYO.

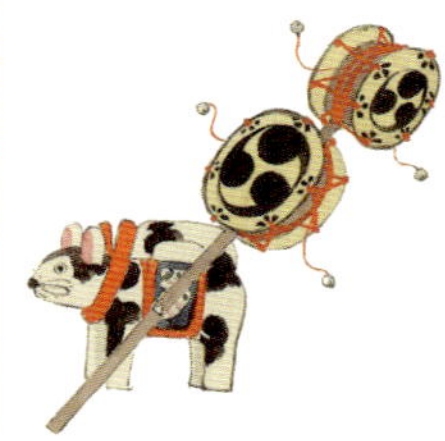

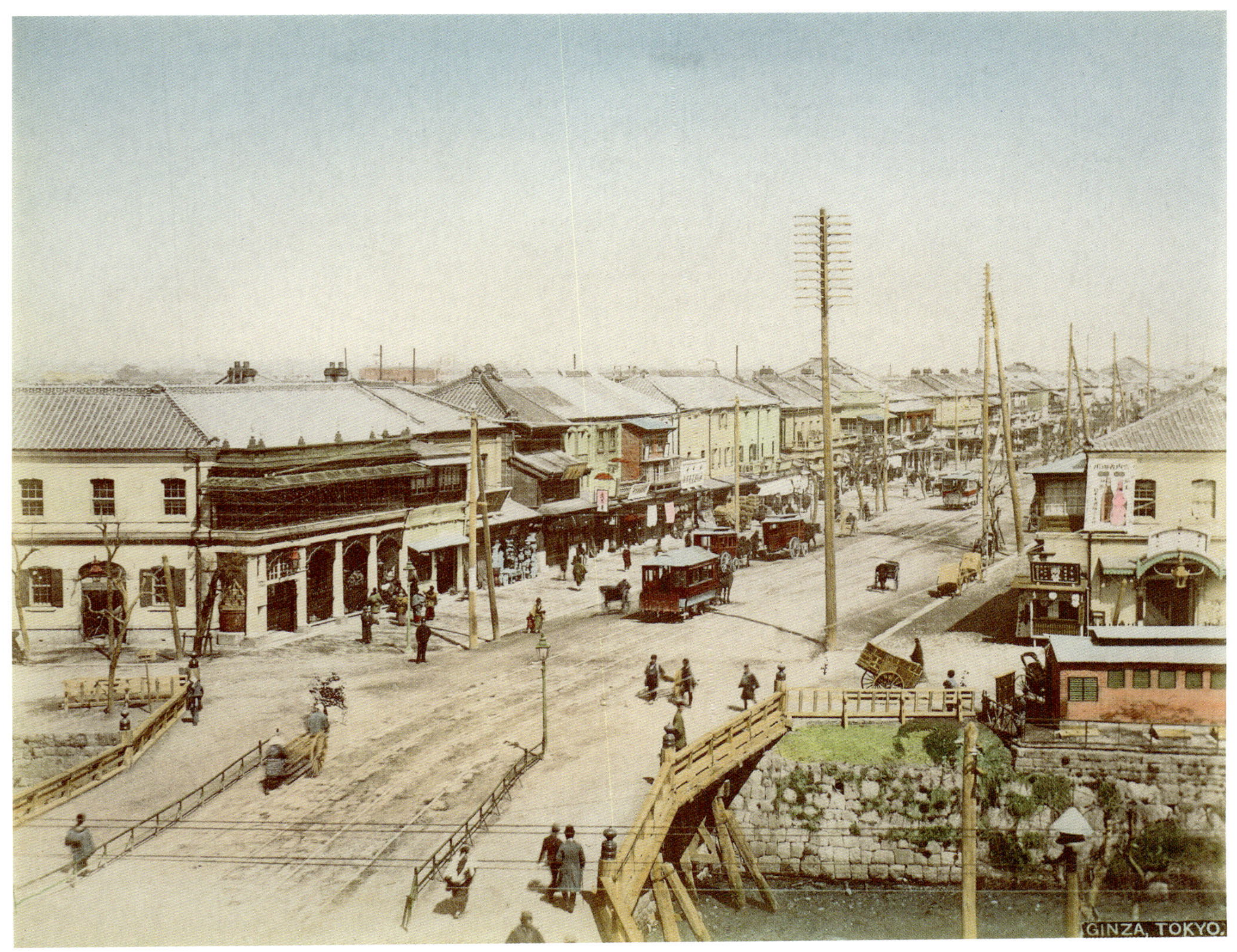

PLATE 21

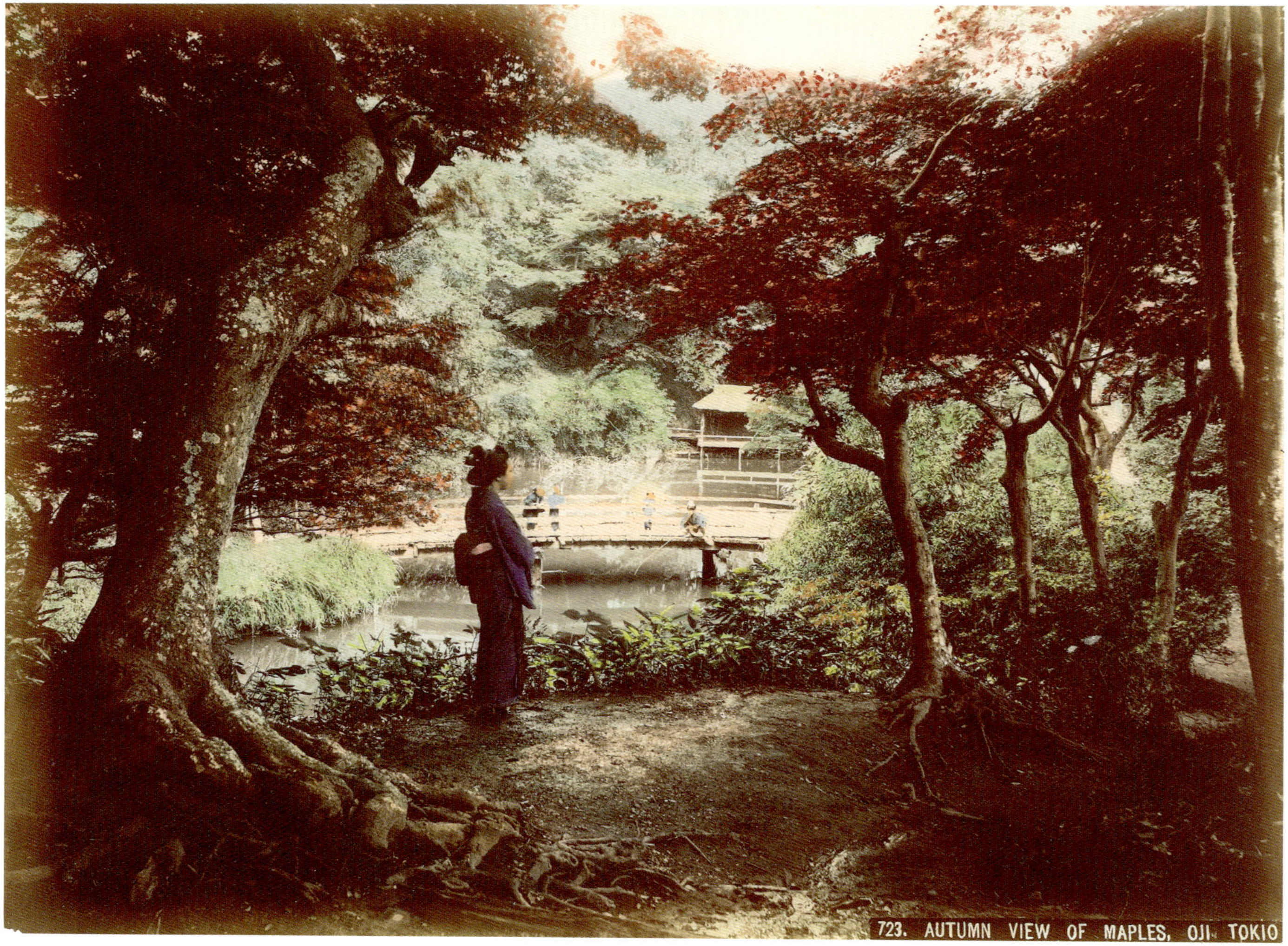

723. AUTUMN VIEW OF MAPLES, OJI TOKIO

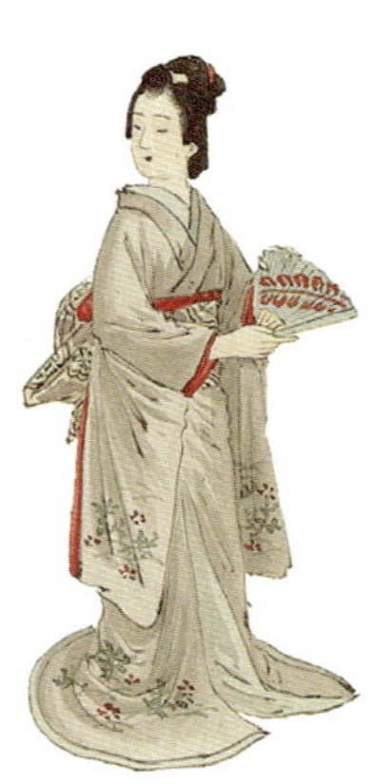

PLATE 22

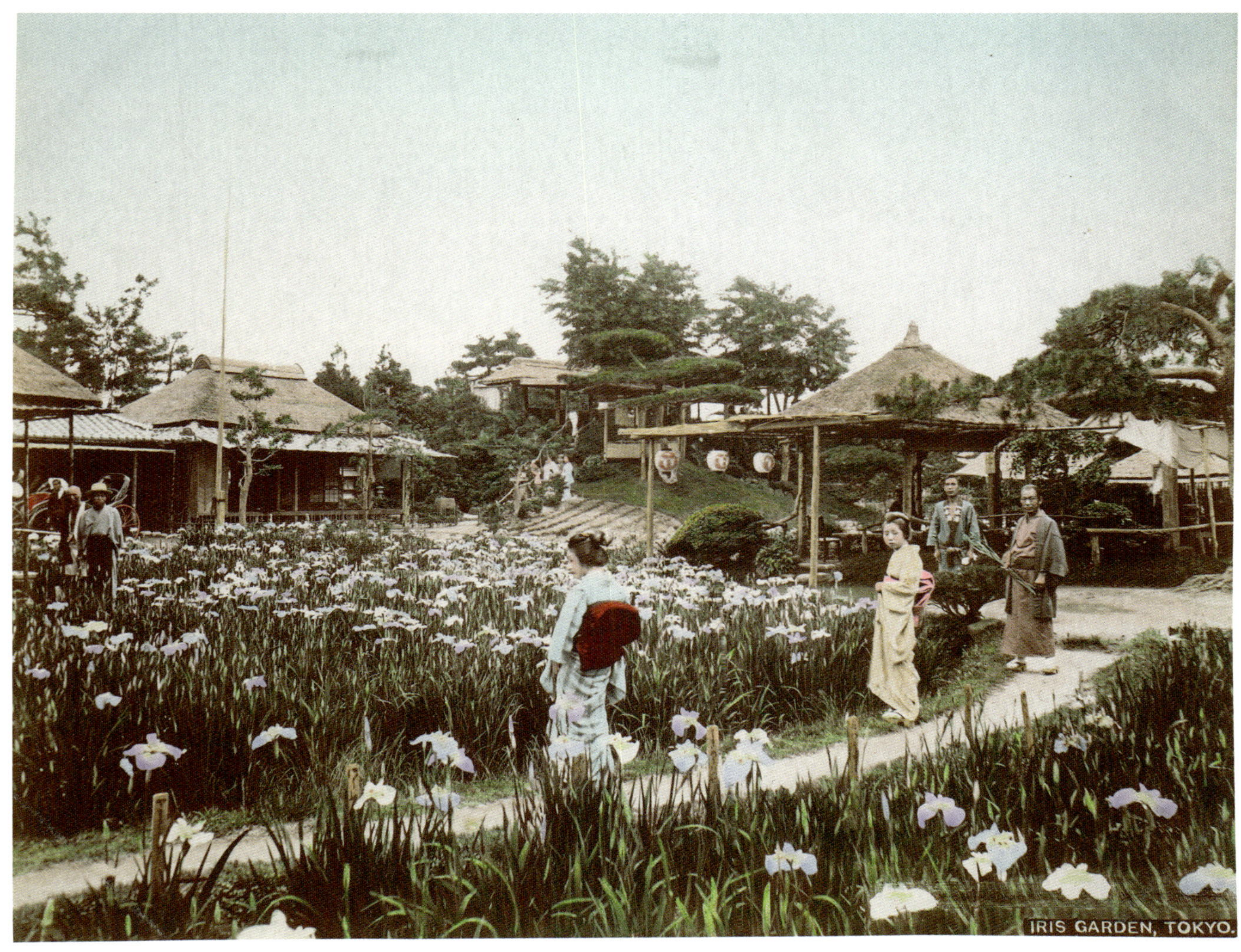
IRIS GARDEN, TOKYO.

PLATE 23

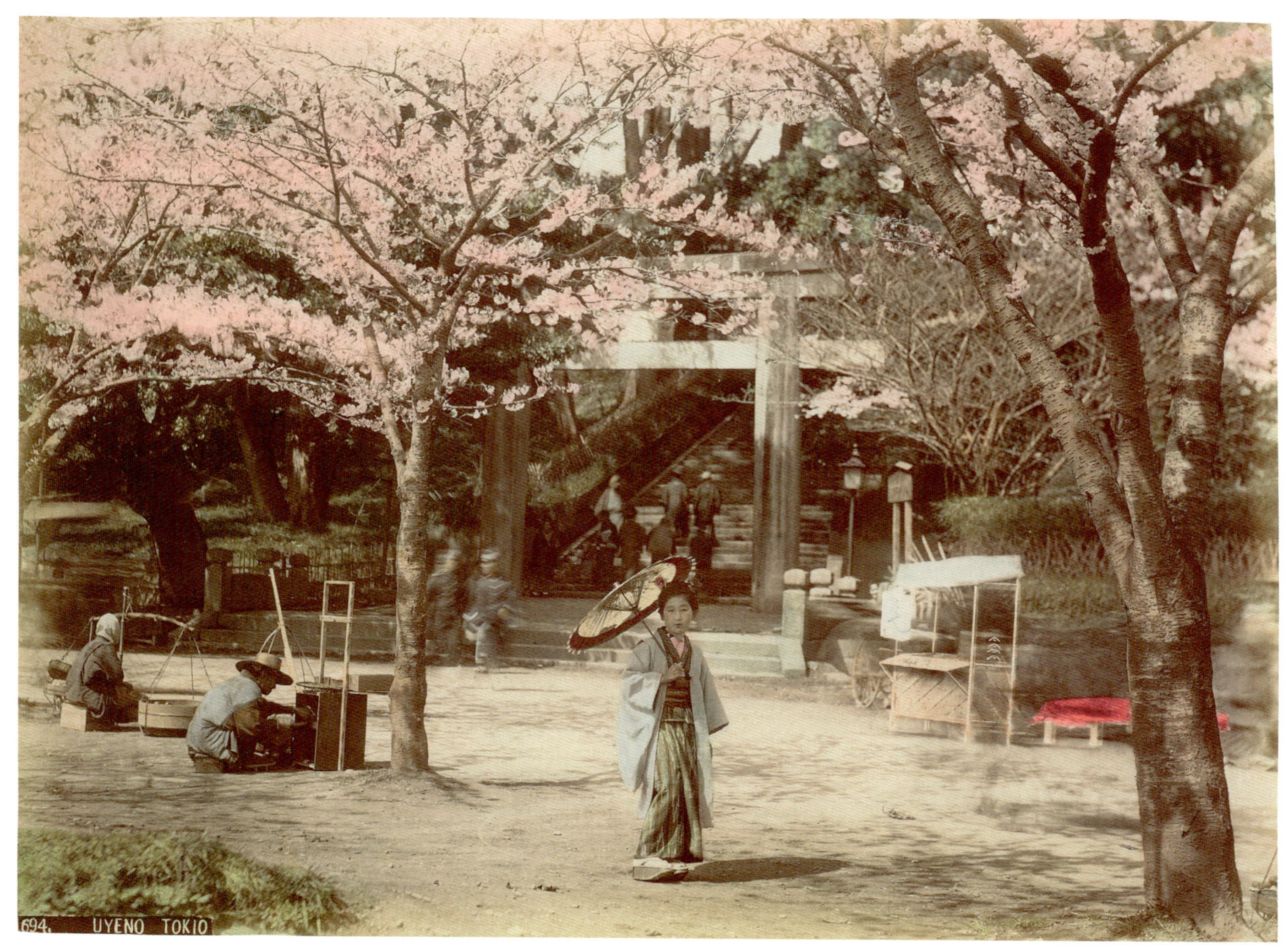

PLATE 24

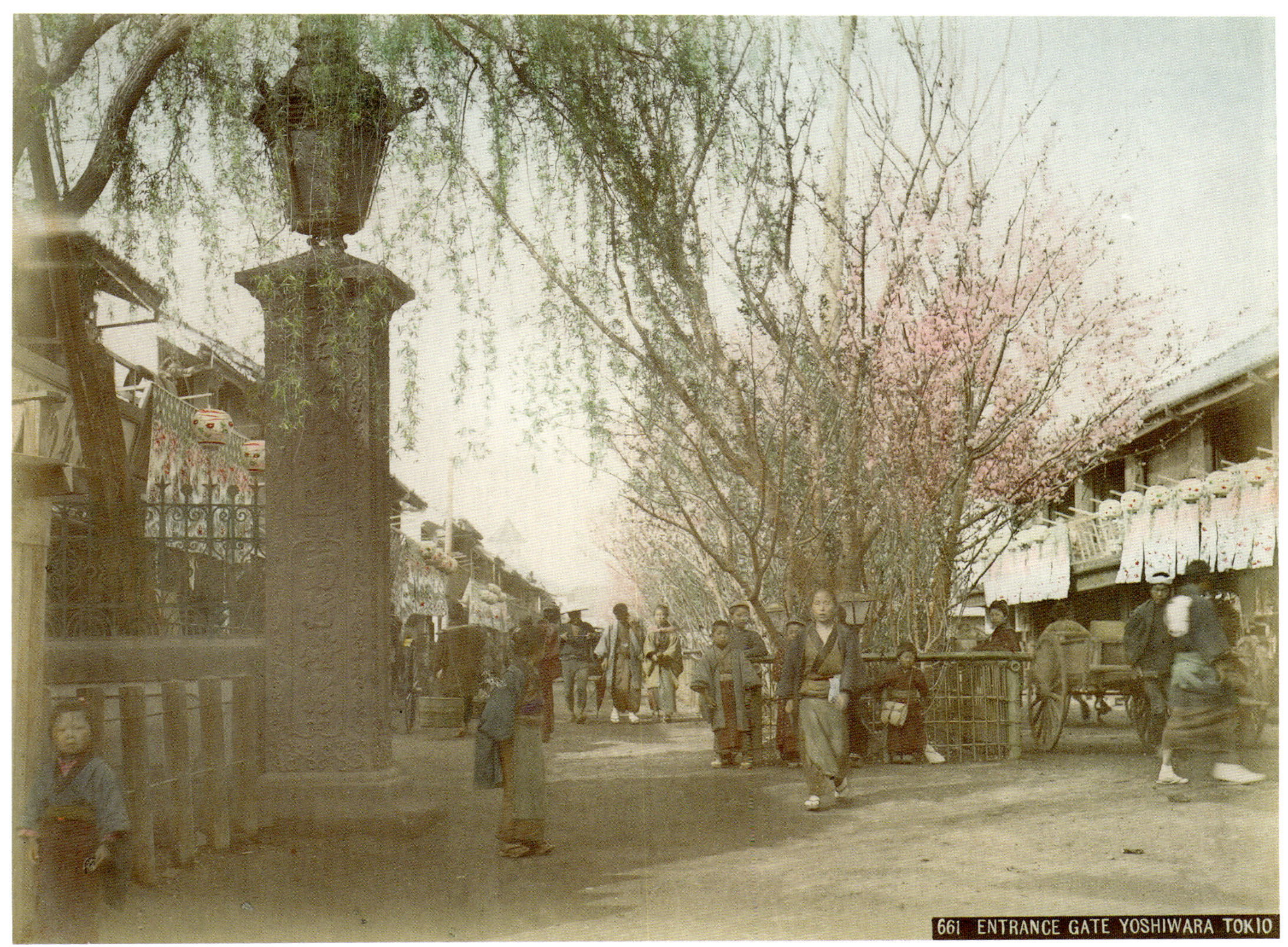

PLATE 25

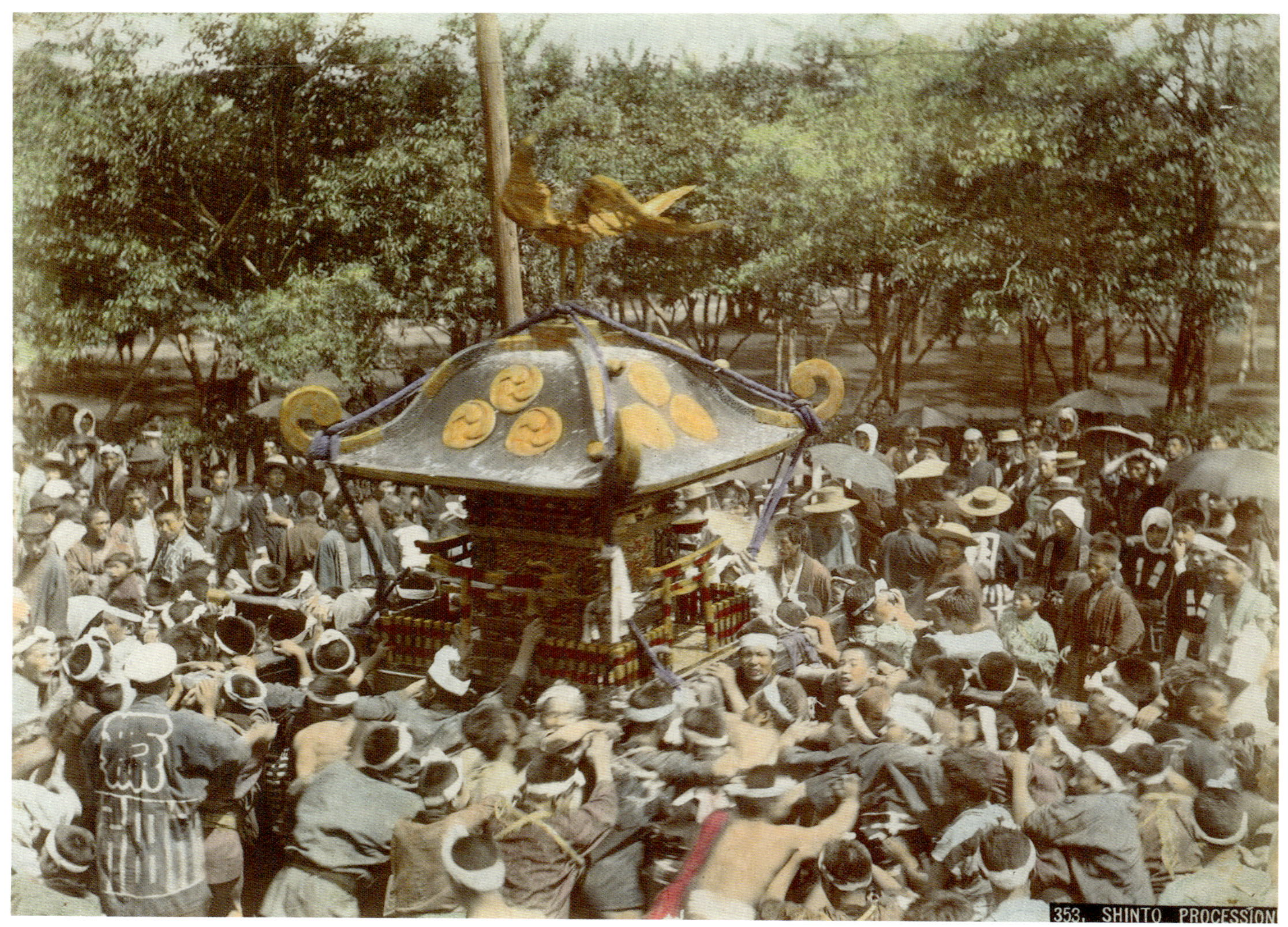

PLATE 26

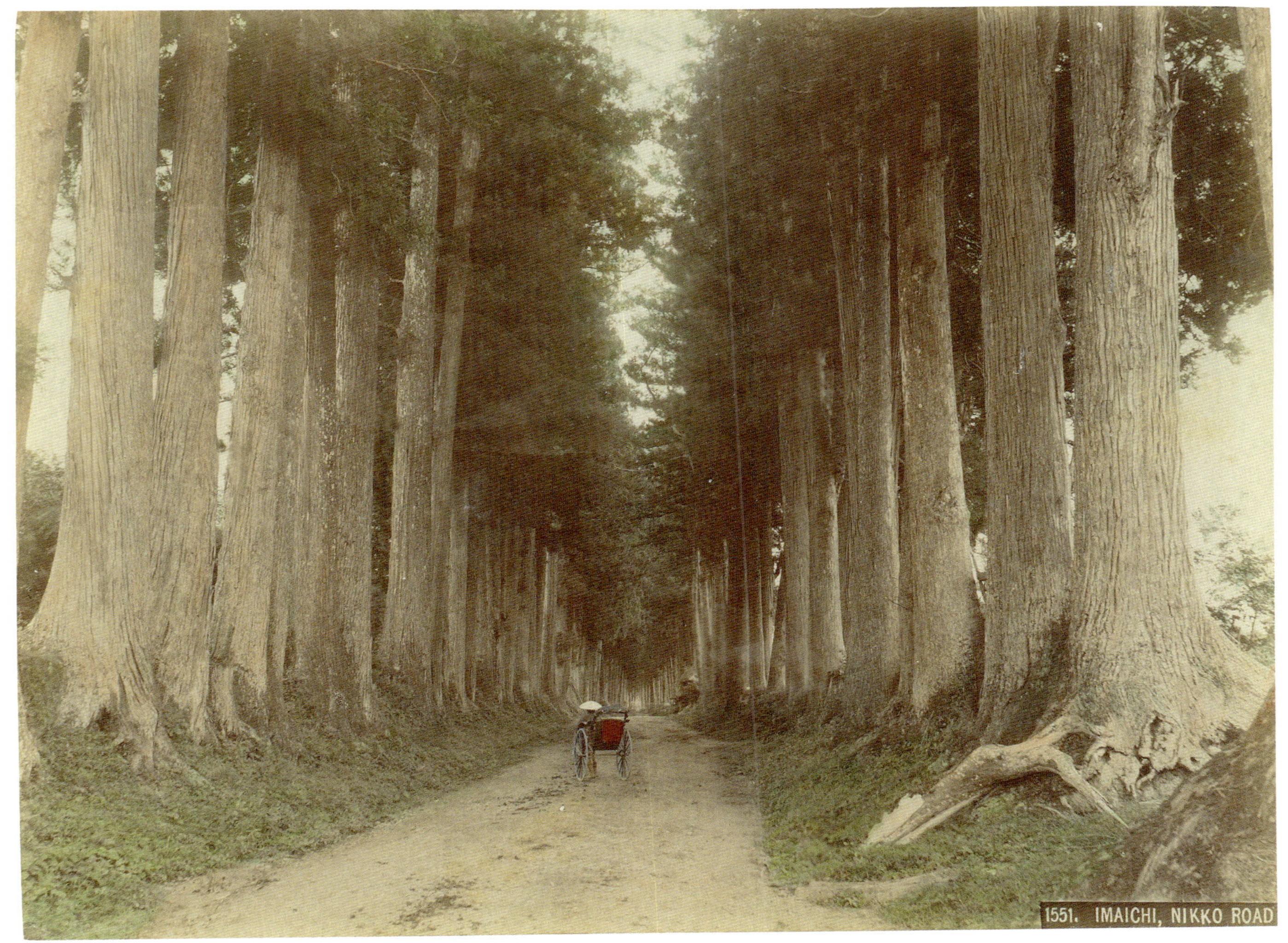

PLATE 27

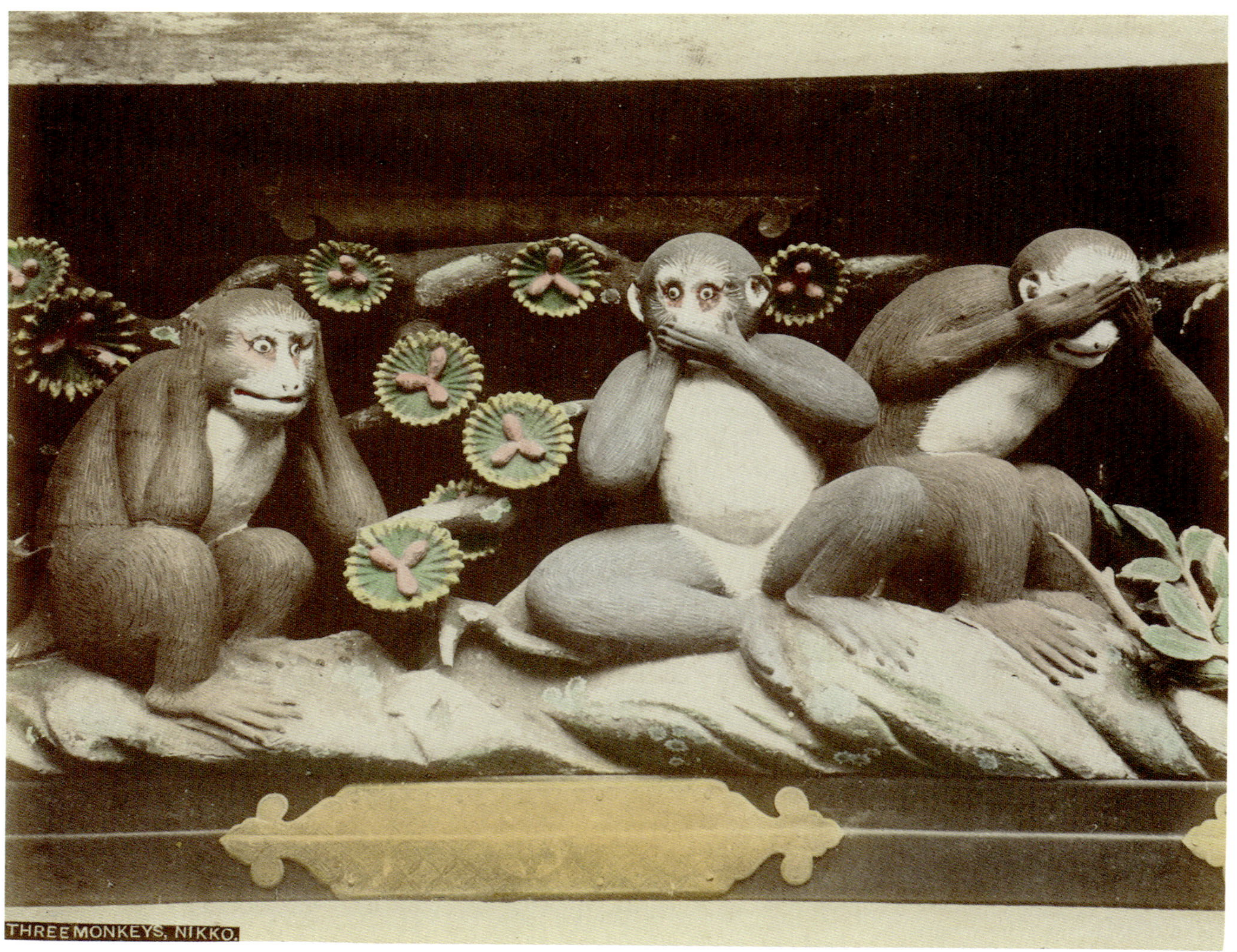

PLATE 28

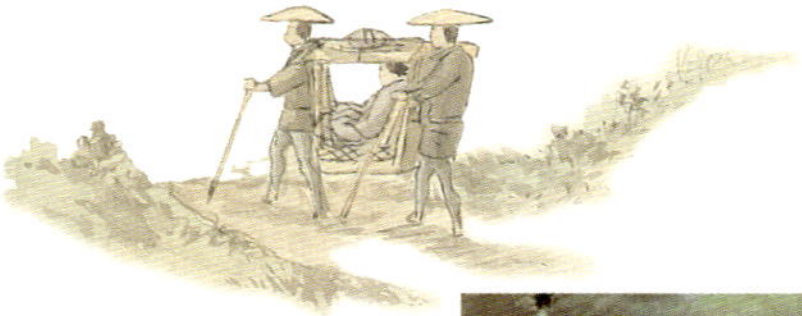

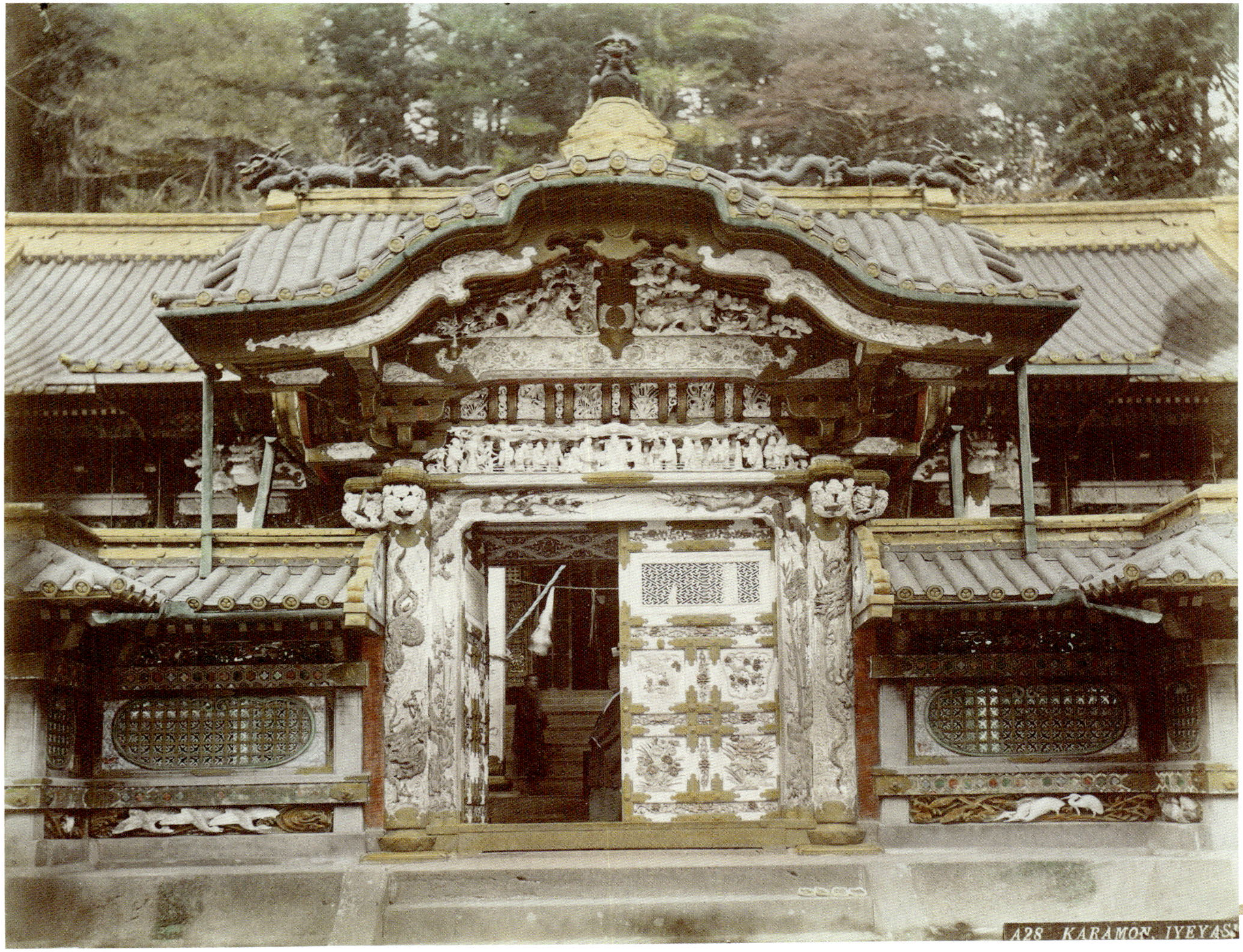

A28 KARAMON. IYEYAS

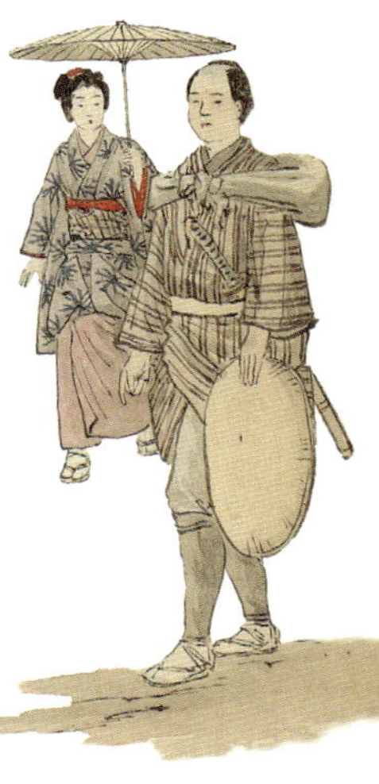

PLATE 29

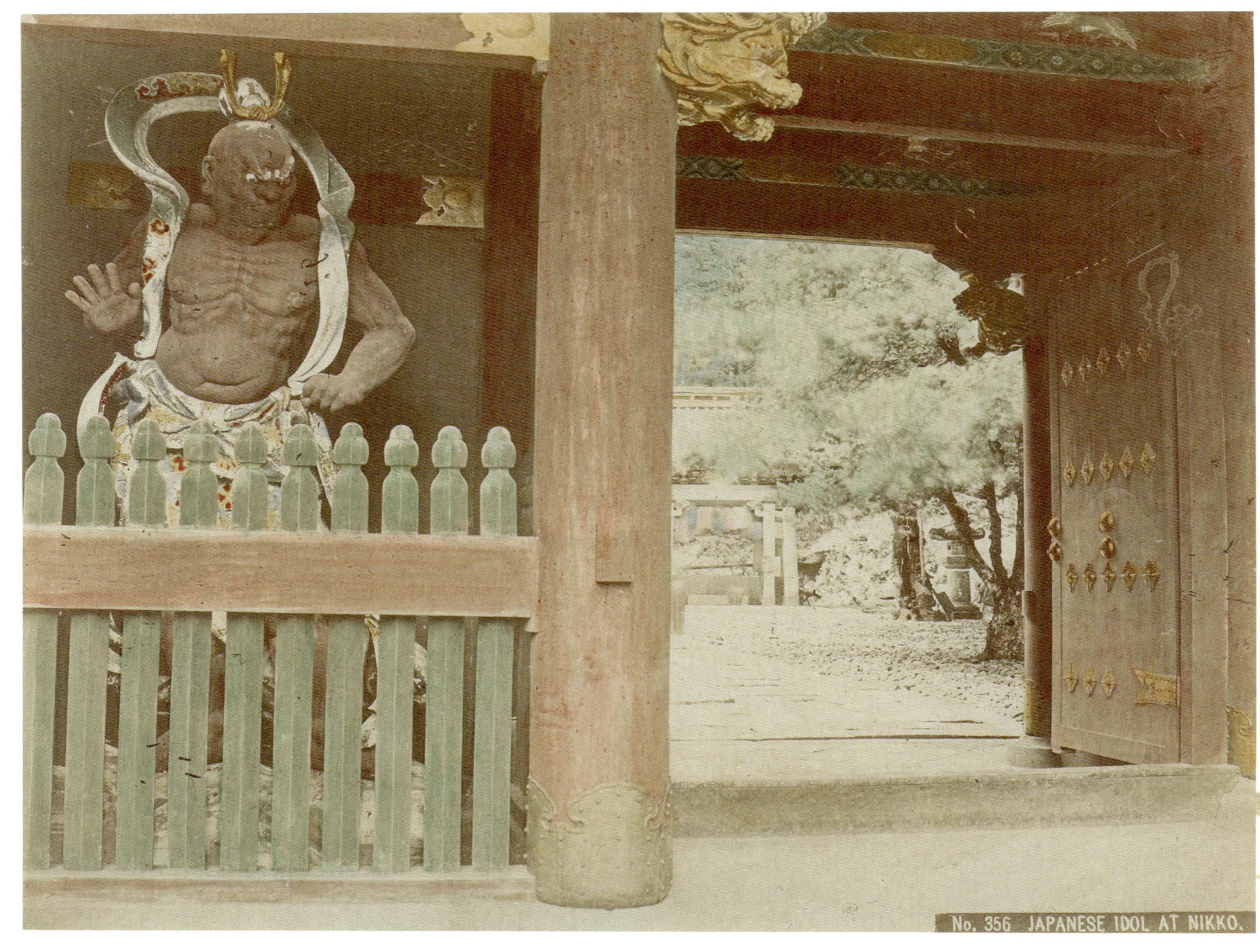

PLATE 30

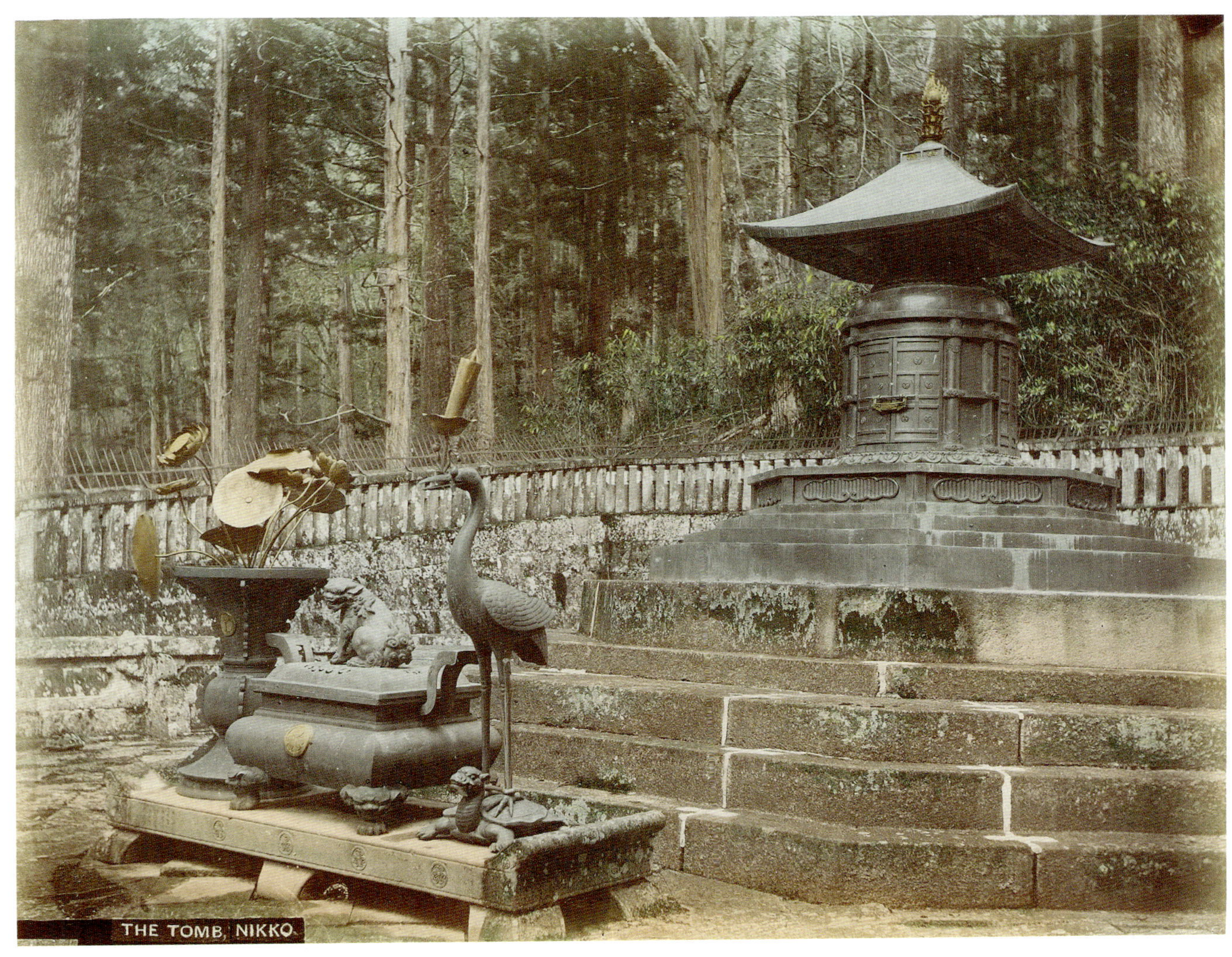

PLATE 31

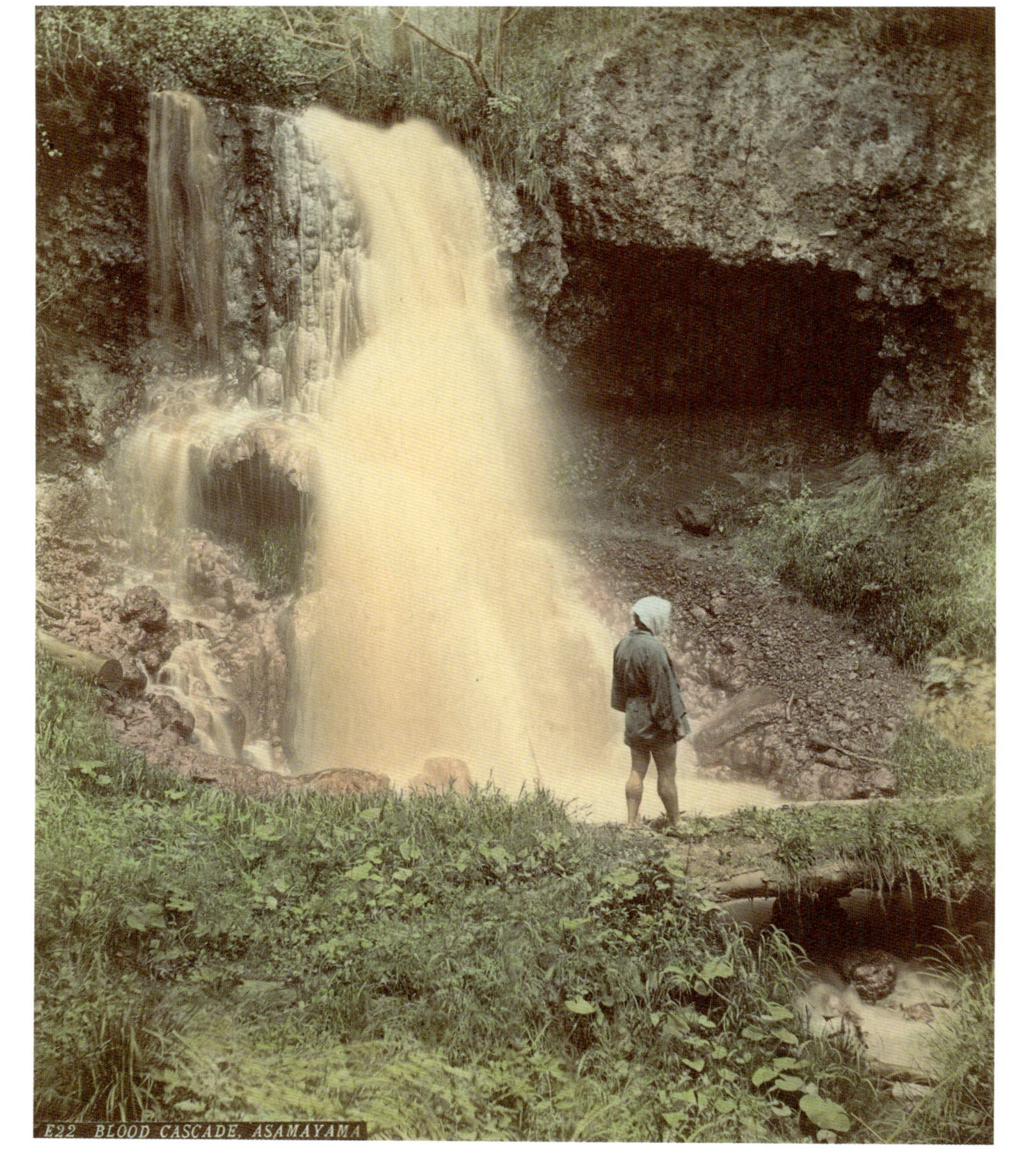

PLATE 32

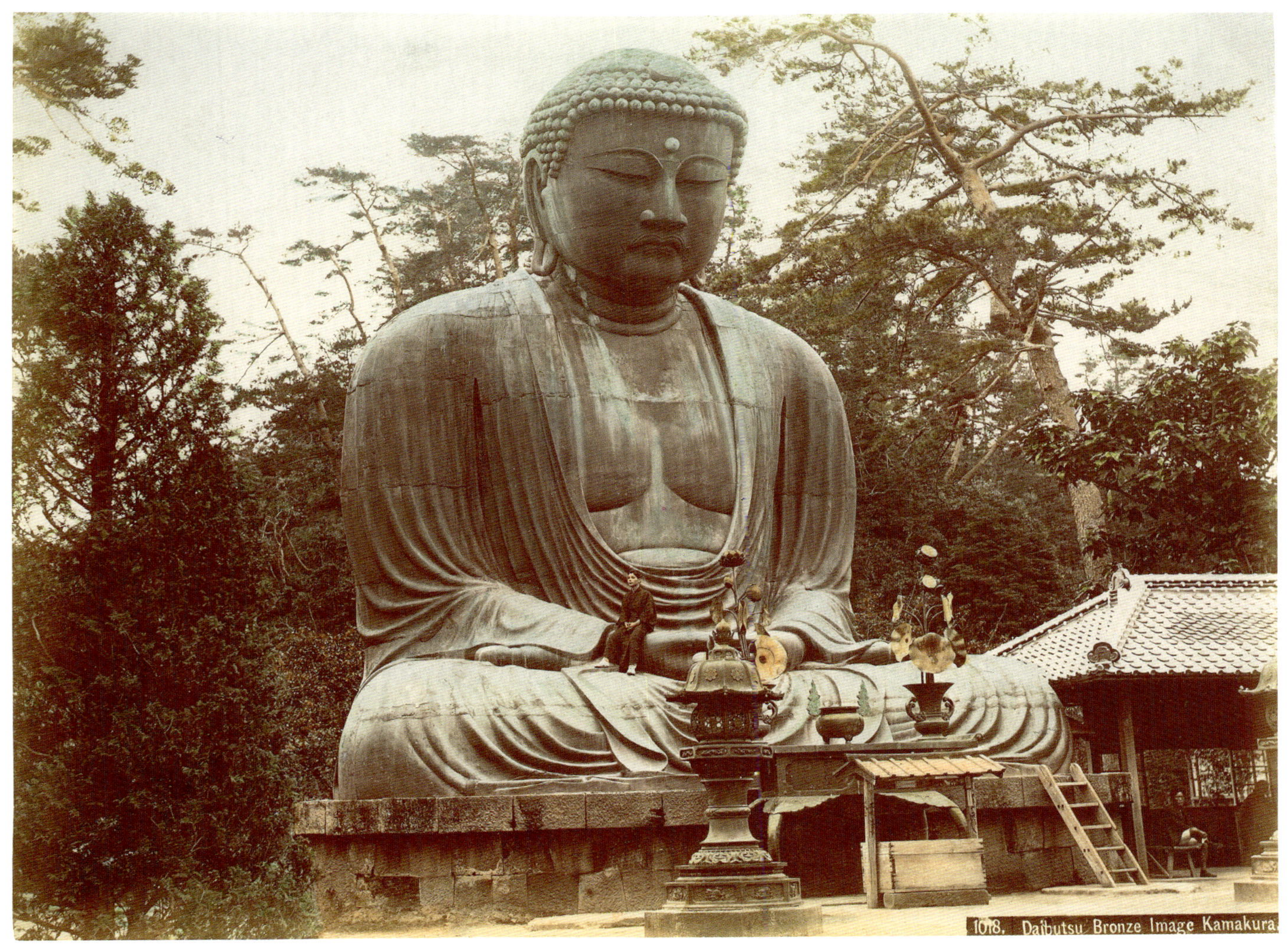

PLATE 33

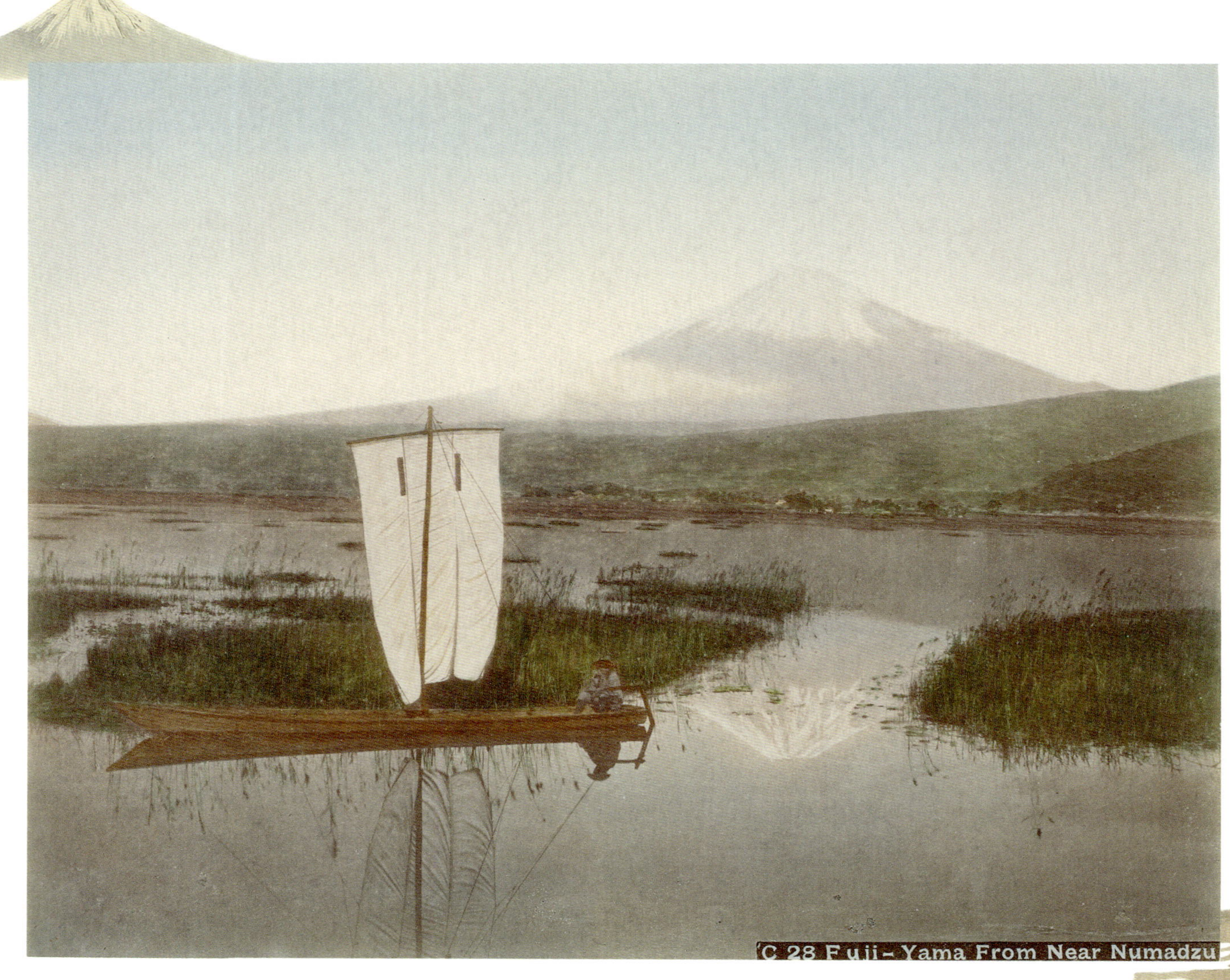

PLATE 34

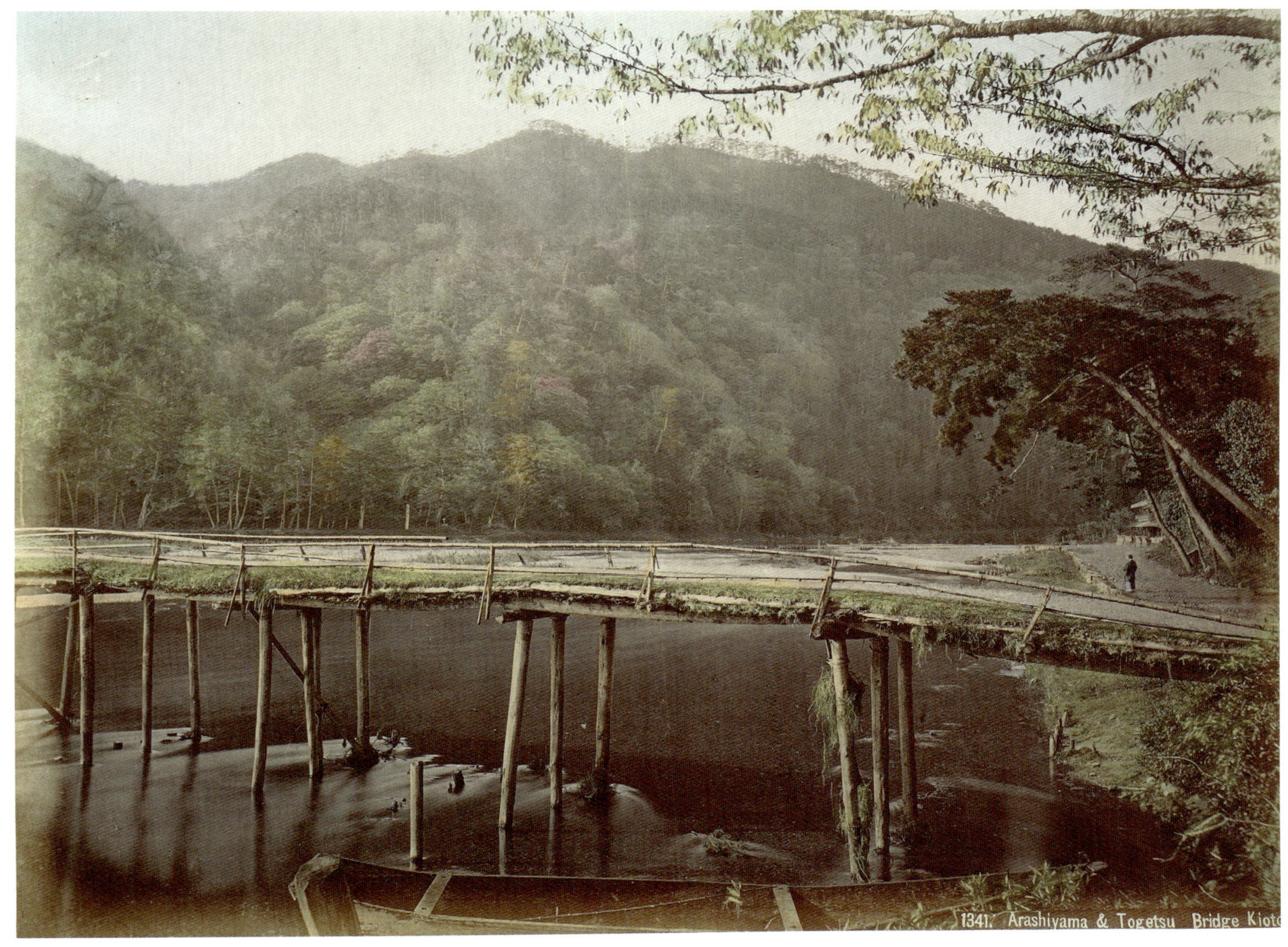

PLATE 35

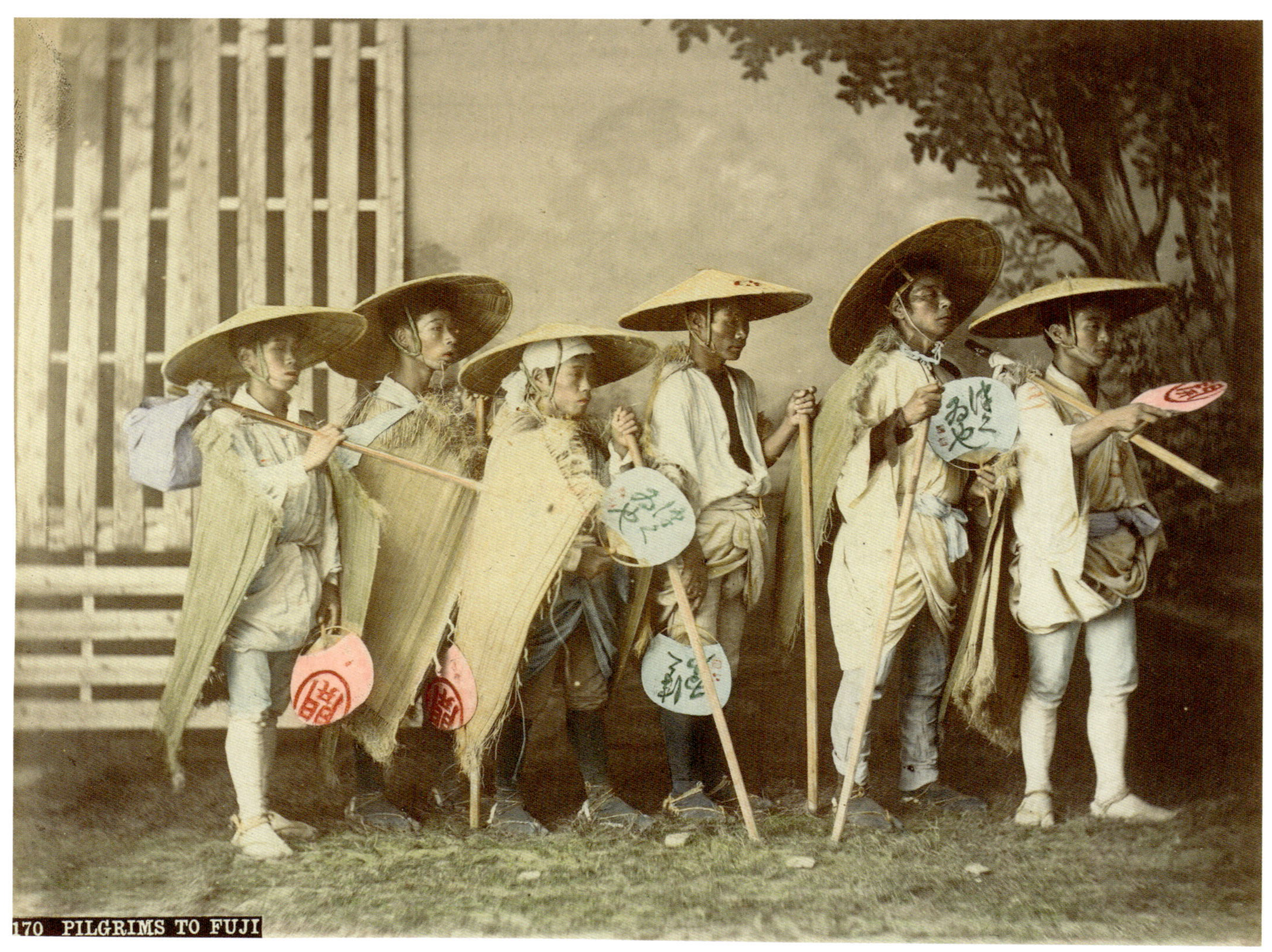

170 PILGRIMS TO FUJI

PLATE 36

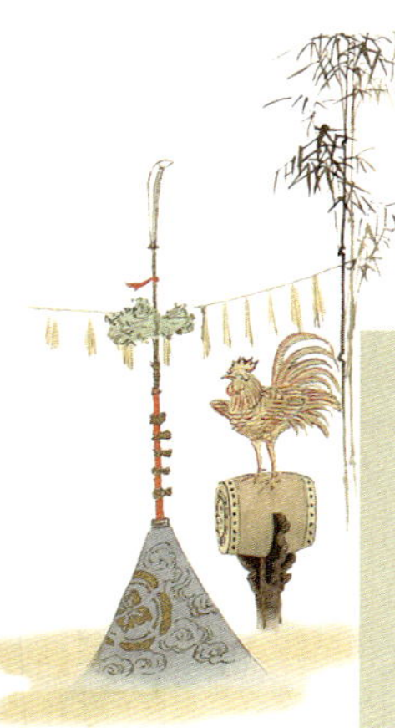

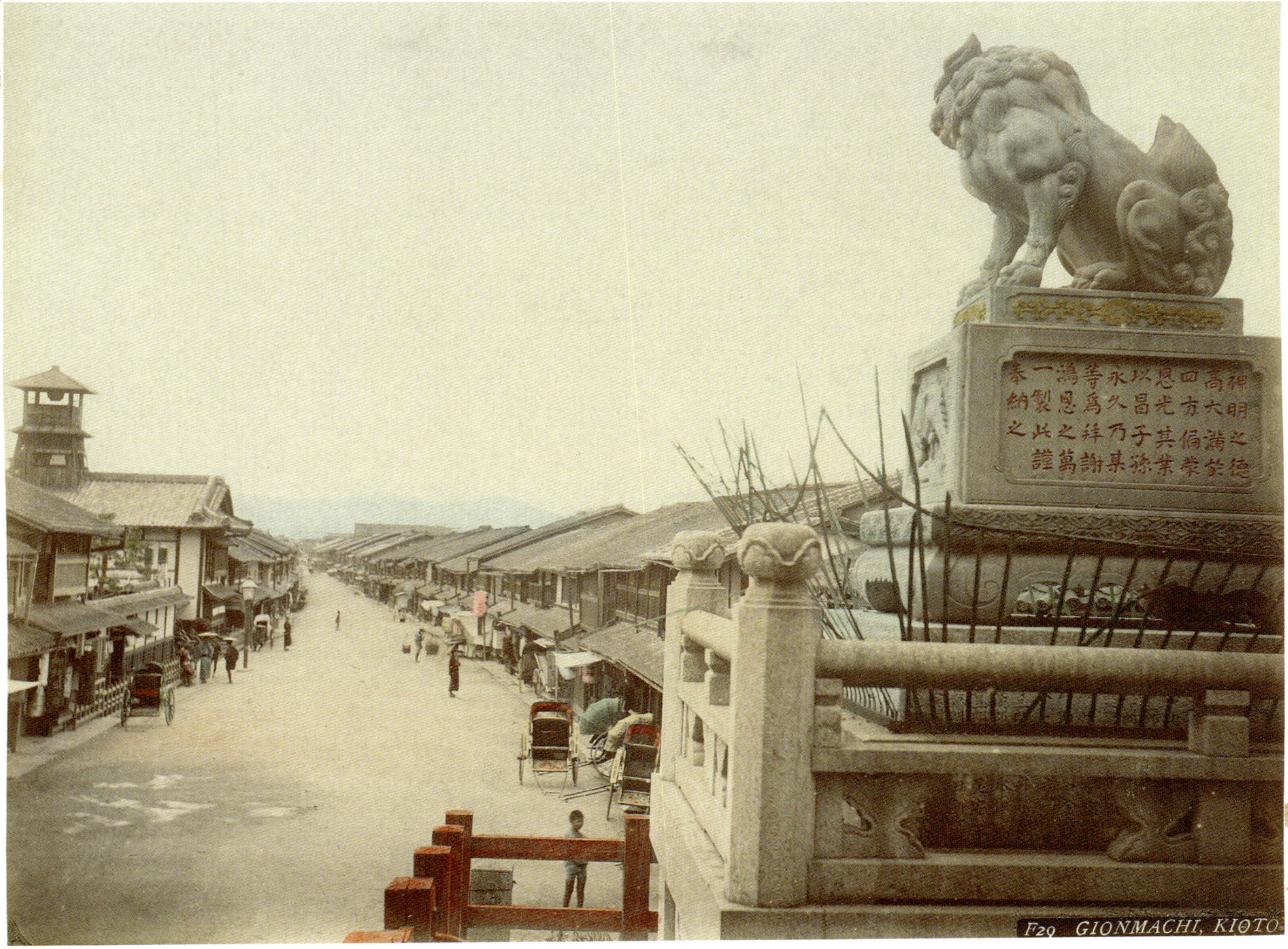

F29 GIONMACHI, KIOTO

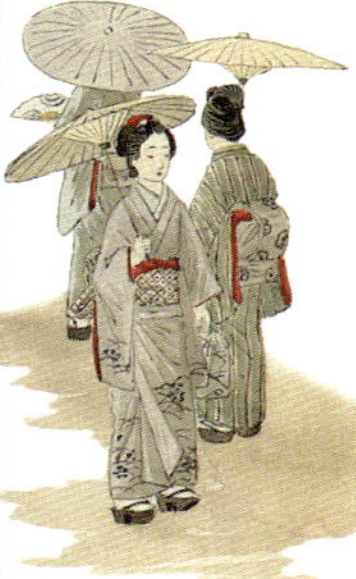

PLATE 37

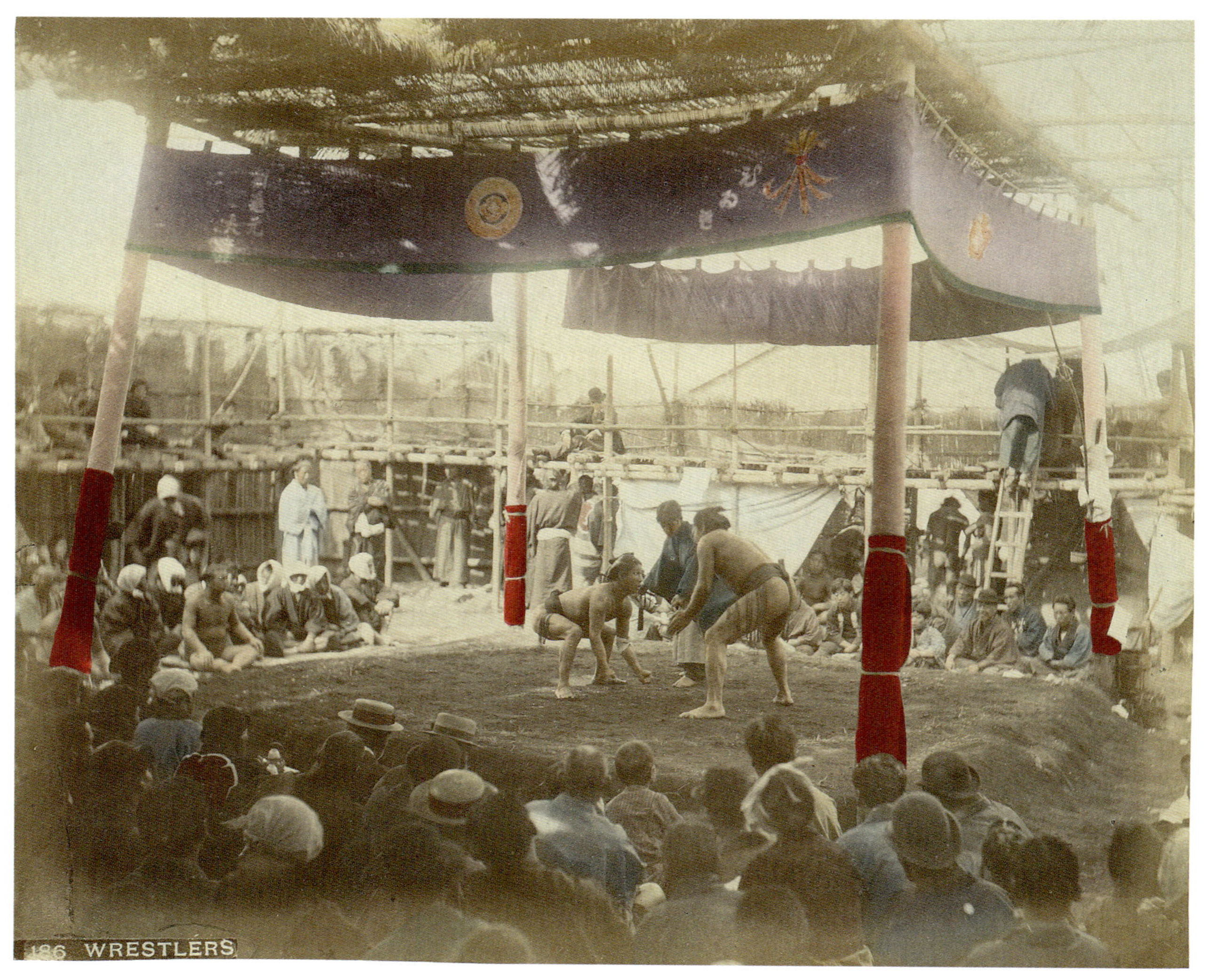

PLATE 38

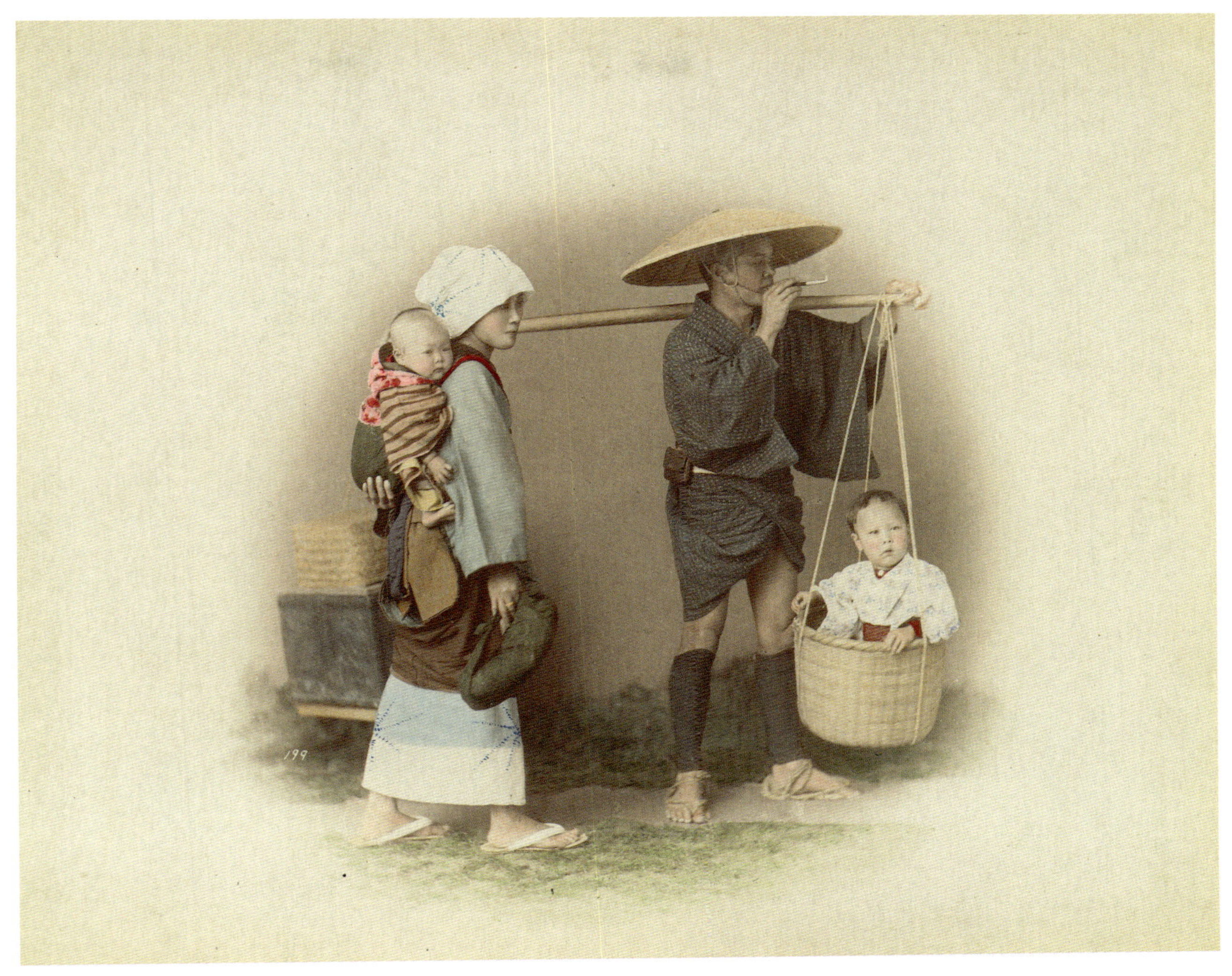

PLATE 39

List of Works

All objects listed below are gifts of Jean S. and Frederic A. Sharf to the Museum of Fine Arts, Boston, unless stated otherwise.

PLATES

1.
Ichida Sōta I (1843–1896)
View of Osaka from Yodogawa, about 1875
Albumen print
20.8 x 27.8 cm

2.
Unidentified Photographer
View of a monumental bell at Hōkōji, Kyoto, about 1875
Albumen print
20.8 x 27.8 cm

3.
Unidentified Photographer
View of Yasaka Shrine, Kyoto, about 1875
Albumen print
20.8 x 27.8 cm

4.
Unidentified Photographer
View of Kinkakuji, Kyoto, about 1875
Albumen print
20.8 x 27.8 cm

5.
Unidentified Photographer
Woman in jinrikisha, about 1875
Albumen print
20.8 x 27.8 cm

6.
Unidentified Photographer
Female dancer and musicians, about 1875
Albumen print
20.8 x 27.8 cm

7.
Unidentified Photographer
*Lady in palanquin (*kago*) with maid and carriers*, about 1875
Albumen print
20.8 x 27.8 cm

8.
Unidentified Photographer
View of a garden, about 1875
Albumen print
20.8 x 27.8 cm

9.
Unidentified Photographer
Western travelers with the head priest of Manganji at Yōmeimon, Tōshōgu Shrine, Nikkō, 1881
Albumen print
20.8 x 27.8 cm
The New York doctor Albert Leffingwell received a print of this photograph from one of the sitters, a young Boston merchant called French, whom he met during his journey to Nagasaki in October 1881. Leffingwell noted in his diary that "he was very entertaining . . . told me of his experiences at Nikko when he succeeded in getting the Bishop of Mangwanji to stand in a group for his photograph arrayed in all his pontifical robes—almost as great a feat as for a Protestant to obtain a like favor from a European Catholic prelate."

10.
Unidentified Photographer
View of a graveyard, about 1875
Albumen print
20.8 x 27.8 cm

11.
Ichida Sōta I (1843–1896)
View of Ishiyama Temple, about 1875
Albumen print
20.8 x 27.8 cm

12.
Tamamura Kōzaburō (1856–?)
View of the roadstead at Yokohama, about 1895
Hand-tinted albumen print
19 x 24 cm

13.
Tamamura Kōzaburō (1856–?)
View of the Bund, Yokohama, about 1895
Hand-tinted albumen print
19 x 24 cm
The Grand Hotel and its recent extension, completed in 1890, dominate the right-hand side of this view of the Bund.

14.
Tamamura Kōzaburō (1856–?)
View of the Grand Hotel, Yokohama, about 1895
Hand-tinted albumen print
19 x 24 cm
This photograph shows the entrance to the extension to the Grand Hotel, viewed from the landward-facing side on Mizumachidōri ("Water Street").

15.
Tamamura Kōzaburō (1856–?)
View of Bentendōri, Yokohama, looking from Sanchōme towards Yonchōme, about 1895
Hand-tinted albumen print
19 x 24 cm

16.
Kusakabe Kimbei (1841–1934)
View of Western-style house on the Bluff, Yokohama, about 1890
Hand-tinted albumen print
20 x 26.5 cm

17.
Tamamura Kōzaburō (1856–?)
Edō Castle, looking from Nijūbashi Moat towards Hamaguri Moat, Tokyo, about 1895
Hand-tinted albumen print
19 x 24 cm

18.
Tamamura Kōzaburō (1856–?)
View of cherry blossoms at Mukōjima on the Sumida River, Tokyo, about 1895
Hand-tinted albumen print
19 x 24 cm

19.
Tamamura Kōzaburō (1856–?)
View of the Ryōunkaku (Twelve-Storied Tower) at Asakusa Park, Tokyo, about 1895
Hand-tinted albumen print
19 x 24 cm

20.
Tamamura Kōzaburō (1856–?)
View of the Nakamise, Asakusa, about 1895
Hand-tinted albumen print
19 x 24 cm

21.
Tamamura Kōzaburō (1856–?)
View of Shinbashi from Ginza, Tokyo, about 1895
Hand-tinted albumen print
19 x 24 cm
From 1882 to 1903, horse-drawn trolleys operated between Nihonbashi and Shinbashi along the main Ginza artery. Later, they were superceded by electric streetcars. The wooden bridge shown here was replaced with an iron bridge in 1899.

22.
Kusakabe Kimbei (1841–1934)
Maples at Takinogawa, Ōji, near Tokyo, about 1895
Hand-tinted albumen print
20 x 26.5 cm
Takinogawa was a popular beauty spot in the Edo period, celebrated for its maples during the fall, and as the shogun's hunting ground for the rest of the year. In 1873, the area was designated a public park.

23.
Tamamura Kōzaburō (1856–?)
Iris at Horikiri, Tokyo, about 1895
Hand-tinted albumen print
19 x 24 cm

24.
Kusakabe Kimbei (1841–1934)
View of Ueno Park, Tokyo, about 1890
Hand-tinted albumen print
20 x 26.5 cm

25.
Kusakabe Kimbei (1841–1934)
View of the Ōmon (Main Gate) to the Yoshiwara Pleasure Quarter, Tokyo, about 1890
Hand-tinted albumen print
20 x 26.5 cm
The iron pillar on the left was one of a pair erected at the entrance to the Yoshiwara quarter in 1881.

26.
Kusakabe Kimbei (1841–1934)
Revelers carrying a mikoshi *(portable palanquin shrine) during a festival*, about 1890
Hand-tinted albumen print
19.5 x 26 cm

27.
Kusakabe Kimbei (1841–1934)
View of the Nikkōkaidō (Nikkō Road) at Imaichi, about 1890
Hand-tinted albumen print
20.2 x 26.4 cm

28.
Tamamura Kōzaburō (1856–?)
Study of the Three Monkeys sculpture, Tōshōgu Shrine, Nikkō, about 1895
Hand-tinted albumen print
19 x 24 cm

29.
Adolfo Farsari (1841–1898)
View of the Karamon (Chinese Gate) at Tōshōgu Shrine, Nikkō, about 1886
Hand-tinted albumen print
19 x 24 cm

30.
Tamamura Kōzaburō (1856–?)
View of the Niōmon at Taiyūin, Rinnōji, Nikkō, about 1890
Hand-tinted albumen print
20 x 26 cm
Taiyūin was established as a mausoleum to the third Tokugawa shogun, Iemitsu.

31.
Tamamura Kōzaburō (1856–?)
View of the mausoleum of Shogun Tokuagawa Ieyasu, Tōshōgu Shrine, Nikkō, about 1895
Hand-tinted albumen print
19 x 24 cm

32.
Adolfo Farsari (1841–1898)
View of the Blood Cascade, Mount Asama, a popular sight on the Nakasendō, about 1886
Hand-tinted albumen print
24 x 19.5 cm

33.
Kusakabe Kimbei (1841–1934)
View of the Daibutsu (Great Buddha) at Hase, Kamakura, about 1890
Hand-tinted albumen print
20 x 26 cm

34.
Unidentified Photographer
View of Mount Fuji from Kashiwabara, about 1885
Hand-tinted albumen print
19 x 24 cm

35.
Kusakabe Kimbei (1841–1934)
View of Togetsu Bridge at Arashiyama, near Kyoto, about 1890
Hand-tinted albumen print
20 x 26.5 cm

36.
Adolfo Farsari (1841–1898)
Group of pilgrims, about 1886
Hand-tinted albumen print
19 x 24.3 cm

37.
Adolfo Farsari (1841–1898)
View of Shijōdōri, Kyoto, about 1886
Hand-tinted albumen print
19 x 24.7 cm

38.
Adolfo Farsari (1841–1898)
Sumō wrestlers, about 1886
Hand-tinted albumen print
20 x 24.3 cm

39.
Adolfo Farsari (1841–1898)
Traveling family, about 1886
Hand-tinted albumen print
20 x 24.5 cm

FIGURE ILLUSTRATIONS

PAGE 9 (left; detail of plate 13)
Tamamura Kōzaburō (1856–?)
View of the Bund, Yokohama, about 1895
Hand-tinted albumen print
19 x 24 cm

PAGE 9 (right)
Adolfo Farsari (1841–1898)
Women in jinrikisha, about 1886
Hand-tinted albumen print on decorated album page
30.5 x 37.5 cm

PAGE 10 (left; same as plate 15)
Tamamura Kōzaburō (1856–?)
View of Bentendōri, Yokohama, looking from Sanchōme towards Yonchōme, about 1895
Hand-tinted albumen print
19 x 24 cm

PAGE 10 (right)
Unidentified Photographer
View of Motomachi Nichōme, looking towards the temple of Zōtakuin, Yokohama, about 1900
Hand-tinted albumen print
19.8 x 25 cm

PAGE 12 (top)
Lacquer photograph album cover from an unidentified Yokohama studio, possibly that of Hagiwara Kisaburō (active 1899–1912)
27 x 36 x 5 cm

PAGE 12 (bottom)
Lacquer photograph album cover from the studio of Adolfo Farsari (1841–1898), about 1890
32 x 40 x 5 cm

PAGE 13
Kusakabe Kimbei (1841–1934)
View of the Fujiya Hotel, Miyanoshita, about 1890
Hand-tinted albumen print
19.8 x 25 cm

PAGE 17
Charles Wirgman (1832–1891)
"Album Thermometer of Count Collodion's affection for his friends..."
Caricature of the photographer Felice Beato (1833 or 34–?), *Japan Punch*, June 1869
Courtesy of Sebastian Dobson

PAGE 18
Uchida Kuichi (1843–1875)
Pleasure boat on the Sumida River near Mukōkima, Tokyo, originally taken about 1872 and reissued by Kusakabe Kimbei about 1885
Hand-tinted albumen print
Courtesy of Sebastian Dobson

PAGE 19
Kusakabe Kimbei (1841–1934)
Pleasure boat on the Sumida River near Mukōjima, Tokyo, about 1890
Hand-tinted albumen print
19.8 x 25 cm

PAGE 22
Charles Wirgman (1832–1891)
"'Farce it is, begorra!!'"
Caricature of David Welsh (active 1870s–about 1892) of the Yokohama Photographic Company, *Japan Punch*, February 1885
Courtesy of Sebastian Dobson

PAGE 24
Adolfo Farsari (1841–1898)
View of Gojōsaka, Kyoto, about 1886
Hand-tinted albumen print
19.5 x 24.5 cm

PAGE 25
Adolfo Farsari (1841–1898)
Laborers in straw rainwear, about 1885
Hand-tinted albumen print
19.5 x 24.5 cm

PAGE 26
Adolfo Farsari (1841–1898)
Decorated album pages with hand-tinted albumen prints, about 1887
Each page 30.5 x 37.5 cm

PAGE 29
Kusakabe Kimbei (1841–1934)
Portrait of a woman, about 1890
Hand-tinted albumen print
19.8 x 25 cm

PAGE 31 (left)
Kusakabe Kimbei (1841–1934)
View of Bentendōri, Yokohama, looking from Nichōme towards Sanchōme, about 1885
Hand-tinted albumen print
19.8 x 25 cm

PAGE 31 (right)
Kusakabe Kimbei (1841–1934)
View of Bentendōri, Yokohama, looking from Nichōme towards Sanchōme and the Kawakita clock tower, 1894
Hand-tinted albumen print
19.8 x 25 cm

PAGE 42
Ryōundō Photographic Studio
View of the Ryōundō Studio near Nunobiki Falls, Kobe, about 1890
Hand-tinted albumen print
Worswick Collection, no. 701
Courtesy of Pacific Press Service, Tokyo and New York

PAGE 43
Tawaraya Sōtatsu (died about 1642)
Nobles viewing the Nunobiki Waterfall, about 1642
Ink, color, and gold on paper
25.1 x 20.6 cm
The John R. Van Derlip Fund, The Minneapolis Institute of Arts, 66.40

PAGE 44
Kano Shōei (1519–1592)
Kiyomizudera from the series *Famous places in the capital and legendary figures*
Fan painting; ink, color, and gold on paper
Width of upper span: 52.4 cm; Width of lower span: 21.2 cm; Height: 19.2 cm
William Sturgis Bigelow Collection, Museum of Fine Arts, Boston, 11.6380c

PAGE 45
Unidentified Photographer
View of Kiyomizudera, Kyoto, about 1890
Hand-tinted albumen print
19.5 x 24.5 cm

PAGE 47 (left)
Katsushika Hokusai (1760–1849)
The surface of the water at Misaka in Kai Province from the series *Thirty-six views of Mount Fuji*, about 1830
Woodblock print; ink and color on paper
25 x 36.9 cm
John T. and William S. Spaulding Collection, Museum of Fine Arts, Boston, 21.5387

PAGE 47 (right)
Utagawa Hiroshige (1797–1858)
The Kinryūzan Temple at Asakusa from the series *One hundred views of Edo*, 1856
Woodblock print; ink and color on paper
36.8 x 24.7 cm
Denman Waldo Ross Collection, Museum of Fine Arts, Boston, 06.639

PAGE 48
Louis Dumoulin (1860–1924)
Carp Banners in Kyoto (formerly known as *Boys' Festival from the Bluff, Yokohama*)
Oil on canvas
46 x 54.3 cm
Fanny Mason Fund in memory of Alice Thevin, Museum of Fine Arts, Boston, 1986.582